Sean Connery

Sean Connery

A BIOGRAPHY BY
KENNETH PASSINGHAM

SIDGWICK & JACKSON
LONDON

First published in 1983 in Great Britain
by Sidgwick and Jackson Limited.

ISBN 0-283-98921-1

Photoset by Robcroft Ltd., London WC1
Printed in Great Britain by
The Garden City Press Limited, Letchworth, Hertfordshire, SG6 1JS
for Sidgwick and Jackson Limited
1 Tavistock Chambers, Bloomsbury Way
London WC1A 2SG

Contents

	List of Illustrations	7
1	Big Tammy	11
2	Body-Building	20
3	Star in the Making	26
4	Hollywood	32
5	Sean Connery is James Bond	38
6	Marriage on the Rock	45
7	Diane Cilento	50
8	From Russia With Love	56
9	The Image Takes Root	62
10	Fighting the Image	68
11	Bondmania	75
12	A Time for Change	81
13	You Only Live Twice	87
14	The Bowler and the Bunnet	93
15	Looking for Something Different	100
16	Work That Appeals	106
17	Back in Bondage	112
18	The Vegas Gamble	118
19	Independent Film-Maker	124
20	A Nightmare of Litigation	131
21	Never Say Never Again	139
	List of Films	143
	Index	155

Illustrations

Between pages 72 and 73

Connery as 'Mr Scotland' bidding to be 'Mr Universe' (*Syndication International*)

Fountainbridge, Edinburgh. The tenement in which Connery used to live has now been pulled down (*Aquarius Film and T.V. Picture Service*)

Darroch Secondary School. 'He was no great scholar. English was the only subject he appeared to be good at' (*Aquarius Film and T.V. Picture Service*)

With Lana Turner in *Another Time, Another Place*, 1958 (*Aquarius Film and T.V. Picture Service*)

On honeymoon with Diane Cilento, 'the girl who has the most inner sex appeal for me', December 1962 (*Syndication International*)

Being fitted for a suit for *From Russia With Love*, March 1963 (*Aquarius Film and T.V. Picture Service*)

With Gert Frobe in *Goldfinger*, 1964 (*Aquarius Film and T.V. Picture Service*)

Diane Cilento and two-year-old Jason. Looking on is Giovanna, aged seven, April 1965 (*Syndication International*)

A scene from *The Hill*, 1965 (*Aquarius Film and T.V. Picture Service*)

Between pages 120 and 121

Bathtime during *You Only Live Twice*, 1966 (*Syndication International*)

Sucking a sea-urchin sting from Claudine Auger's foot in *Thunderball*, 1965 (*Syndication International*)

A scene from *Zardoz*, 1974 (*David Stein/Scope Features*)

With Brooke Adams during filming of *Cuba*, 1979 (*Photographers International*)

With his wife Micheline, March 1981 (*Betty Burke Galella*)

With son Jason in August 1982 (*Syndication International*)

Sean Connery

1
Big Tammy

The scent and smoke and sweat of the Lothian billiards hall this night was compounded into a compost of nervous tension tinged with fear and greed. Members of the Valdor gang who had imprinted their notoriety on certain citizens had decided to pay a visit. It was not exactly social. It was not even to cue the odd ball about the baize. Most of those present knew that when these tearaways paid a visit their calling card usually came in the ugly shape of a razor, a length of bicycle chain or a piece of rubber hose weighted with lead.

Glasgow may have been Scotland's meanest city, but in Edinburgh in the early fifties there was gang warfare on the streets with the Valdors among the toughest predators roaming the Leith area in general and picking out in particular the *palais-de-danse* at Fountainbridge as their natural target. Here what often began as a run-of-the-mill fight would escalate into a near-riot with tables and chairs and their contents being flung over a balcony hovering fifteen feet above the dance floor on to the dancers below.

With their female counterparts known as the Black Angels, girls who wore tight black skirts, equally tight black sweaters, black stockings and black stiletto-heeled shoes, the Valdor gang could create considerable havoc, the girls providing slashing back-up with razor-combs and the heels of their whipped-off shoes as weapons.

To suggest they were less than formidable would be a distinct understatement as sundry assorted scars and brain damage to those unfortunate enough to get in their way bore eloquent testimony. Now, three or four of them were grouping themselves in front of a bench seat on which a jacket had been draped. Its owner, a tall, well-muscled young man in his early twenties known to intimates as 'Big Tammy' was bending over the billiards table about to take his shot when he saw them. He straightened up and, cue in hand, walked across to the bench where one of them was sitting screened by the others.

'Okay,' he said, 'put it back.'

'Put what back?'

'Put back whatever you took from my pocket.'

'I never touched your pocket.'

The big man's hand stretched out, gripping the offender's collar. 'I said put it back.'

The menaced one whined: 'I tell you I haven't got anything.' Opened hands confirmed it, but the big man knew what they were about and that he'd moved too fast for them to take his wallet.

'Okay. Now get away from my jacket. Go on – get going.' A shoulder thrust helped the nearest on his way and the intruders left the hall foul-mouthed and truculent. Big Tammy turned back to the billiards table.

The following night he went to the Fountainbridge *palais-de-danse*. He went there at least a couple of times a week because he fancied girls, loved movement and favoured the quickstep. Which was just as well because this night, as he walked along the balcony above the dance floor, the Valdor gang closed in.

Five or six of them approached, confidently mob-handed.

'Well, if it isn't the bright guy who told us to blow from the billiards hall,' one sneered.

'That's right,' said Big Tammy. 'That's me.'

They moved to encircle him, working him towards the balustrade edging the balcony. He knew that given half a chance they would heave him over. Turning swiftly, he grabbed the two who were behind him, one by the throat, the other by a bicep. He squeezed and jerked them towards one another in one violent movement that cracked their heads together. Hard.

'Now blow,' he said, 'or I'll throw you straight over the balcony.'

Such sudden controlled violence told them he meant it. They not only left. From then on they left Big Tammy, otherwise known as Tommy Connery, strictly alone. He preferred to walk alone because he valued his privacy. He was not to know there was a much higher price to be paid for it until some time later, after he had decided to adapt his boyhood nickname of Shane and call himself Sean. Sean Connery.

He was not to know either, at this moment in his eventful life, that a world and wealth away from cold and wet Edinburgh his future was being irrevocably shaped not by his own actions but by a man who was sitting in his hideaway home on Jamaica's north shore. A home he called, prophetically you may think, Goldeneye. A snob and sophisticate, moulded by his schooling at Eton, educated by travel and honed by Second World War experience as a naval intelligence officer, he was about to write a book as a diversion; a sort of counter-irritant to his alarm at the prospect of getting married for the first time at the age of forty-three.

The man's name was Ian Fleming and he was surveying his bookshelf, wondering what to call the fictional character he had in mind to act out his own fantasies on paper. He was looking for what he thought would sound a flat, quiet name. Glancing through the titles he noted a standard ornithological work: *Birds of the West Indies*. The author: James Bond.

Fleming began to write: 'James Bond suddenly knew he was tired. He always knew when his body or his mind had had enough . . . '

The die was cast: the phenomenon was yet to come.

Poverty, depending on where you find it, has its own peculiar smell. In southern Italy or Spain it smells of heat because there is the sun and you feel you can survive the hunger because you only need something light to wear. In Scotland poverty smells of damp, of the cold and rain that permeates the brickwork of tenement buildings too old to protest and you feel you can survive only if there are clothes on your back and warmth in your belly. It was to such a tenement block, 176 Fountainbridge, in the princely city of Edinburgh that Joseph Connery, a half-Scots half-Irish rubber worker brought his wife Euphemia and Thomas, their first-born, back from the Royal Maternity Hospital where the baby first saw the grey light of day at 6.05 p.m. on 25 August 1930.

Perhaps it is why the most cherished memories of early childhood for Tommy Connery are of holidays spent with his mother's parents in the country air far from the madding overcrowd of that teeming tenement with its paper-thin walls allowing no privacy of thought or speech. There, where the windows overlooked a brewery and a rubber mill, the Connery clan was just one of twelve families sharing what the Scots call 'the stair' and its one communal lavatory.

The Connerys had two rooms, a large kitchen which doubled as the living room, and a bedroom where, as a baby, Sean Connery christened Thomas was tucked up in the long bottom drawer of his parents' wardrobe which served as a cot. When he outgrew this makeshift arrangement he slept in the kitchen on a bed-settee where he was later joined by his brother Neil who was eight years younger. Luxury was when they had separate divans and could enjoy pillow fights. It was no contest. As the younger, weaker and smaller of the two it was Neil who would invariably end up like a trussed chicken, helplessly knotted into a sheet by his brother.

There was no bathroom, and water had to be heated for the bath which was a tin tub in front of the fire. Often when the boys were small their father would bathe them without going to the time-wasting trouble involved in heating the water and filling the tub. He would simply stand them in the sink under running cold water. When their mother protested that the water was too cold he would take no notice. 'Och, awa' wi' you woman,' he'd say as each one wriggled like an eel under the tap, 'it'll do them no harm.'

When they were bigger and old enough they went to the public baths, the municipal 'plunge', where for threepence, sixpence or a shilling they could get a hot bath, the amount of water to luxuriate in being governed by how much money they were prepared to pay. Usually it was sixpence. The soap there was free, but it was of a coarse carbolic about the size of a domino so they would take their own soap and towels for this weekly ritual. When a man earned between £4 and £5 a week, as Tommy Connery's father – now a furniture removal man – did, sixpence seemed a lot of money to pay for a bath. Even though the family housekeeping was boosted by the extra 30 shillings a week their mother earned as an early morning office cleaner. It is why, in later years, Sean Connery would remember the cold and the wet and the constraints of poverty and say: 'I have a great respect for money. I never get over the fact that sometimes I see more money being paid for a meal than my father earned in a week.' And this was said long before inflation made it even more of a mocking comparison.

However, tight as money was, the family did not want for food. What they had was simply enough, but it was nourishing, sustaining and above all, economical. There was no question of having your cake and eating it in the Connery household because Mrs Connery was a thrifty manager who would not buy anything she felt she could do without. Bread and potatoes were cheap enough in those days and there was plenty of milk and porridge, the native broth, Irish stew, fruit and bread-and-butter pudding.

Life was fairly predictable in that neighbourhood where poverty held you a prisoner of the environment. The Union Canal 100 yards away was the fishing ground for tiddlers. The streets were a training ground where you learned to take care of yourself. And an undistinguished plot of wasteland was the battleground where you learned to play football with tightly screwed-up newspapers rolled into a ball. Indeed, from that primitive beginning young Tommy Connery showed an aptitude for the game that in later years impressed club scouts on the look-out for professional talent.

Saturday afternoons were for escape into make-believe, a picture house where for twopence you could see serials like Flash Gordon and those old-fashioned Westerns where the baddies and the goodies were clearly distinguishable in black and white and you knew with certainty whose side you were on.

But the real escape was the freedom from city confinement the brothers discovered in the countryside near Dumfermline where Grandfather and Grandmother McLean, their maternal grandparents, lived in a two-roomed cottage. It was here, during holidays from school, that the boys could run wild in the sur-rounding fields and woodland and finally wend their tired way back to hot scones baked by Granny over an open fire where she cooked fondly remembered meals that made the tastebuds tingle: lambs' hearts, a sheep's head and, on occasion, the traditional haggis.

When he was a baby Grandmother Helen McLean would walk Tammy in his pram to the Rose Garden Park and in later years when her grandson found fame would proudly confide that as a boy he would tell his mother: 'I'm not coming home. I'm staying with Gran!' In the tiny cottage he and his brother slept together in the bedroom while their grandparents slept in the kitchen. In the mornings they washed in pure spring water because there was none on tap and they were given a pitcher by Granny to take down the road to a farm for milk. It came, to their wonderment, delight and initial consternation, still warm from a cow. Once, according to Neil Connery, they tried to milk a cow themselves, believing it would give milk by working its tail up and down like a pump handle. The cow was far from happy and they did not try again.

The farm also yielded newly-laid eggs and they watched in fascination as their grandfather would pierce a hole in an eggshell and suck the contents dry. They too acquired a taste for raw eggs, using their penknives to bore the holes, swallowing down the yolks as richer folk might swallow oysters, regarding them as a delicacy.

For city-bred kids this was the magic of the countryside. There was a pond where they fished for tadpoles, newts and frogs which they would deposit carefully in an old bath in the garden to keep an eye on their progress. They rode a huge Clydesdale horse that was kept on the farm, a gentle giant that waited patiently as they clambered up on to its back and clung to its mane for support. Tommy would first hoist his brother aboard and then try to climb up behind him. This effort usually ended with Neil being unseated, grimly clutching the mane as he slid under the horse's belly.

In such carefree ways the summer holidays passed all too swiftly. It was one winter when he was twelve years old that Tommy Connery had an accident that could have cost him his life. It was an experience to be forever etched on his mind not just because he still bears the terrifying scar of what happened that day but because it brought him, for the first time, face to face with the death of others.

In Edinburgh there was snow on the slopes of an open space known locally as The Meadows. It looked too good just to stand there looking at it. So young Connery built himself a sledge which he painted black and called The Coffin. Maybe it was too great a temptation for fate not to intervene. Tommy took the sledge up the steepest slope and tobogganed down, exhilarated by the sensation of speed. He repeated this several times and then as he hurtled down the hard-packed snow for just one more trip The Coffin skewed at an angle hitting the exposed roots of a tree. The sledge stopped instantly but momentum carried its occupant forward as though slung from a catapult. He met the tree trunk head on.

He was late home that day, having half-walked, half-run with the sledge on his back and a wound that no one noticed at first because he ran into a rocket from his mother. She scolded him for being late for supper and he said nothing about his accident. Then she noticed his pallor.

'Is something wrong?' she asked him.

'It's nothing,' he said. 'I hit my head but it doesn't hurt.'

He went across to wash his hands at the sink and it was then that his mother saw blood running down the back of his neck. She took a piece of clean cloth to wipe the blood away – and the cloth fell in. There was a gaping injury that shocked and horrified her. She almost fainted.

Frantic, she screamed out to a next-door neighbour for help. The neighbour ran to a phone and called for an ambulance. By the time it arrived her son had lost a great deal of blood. At the hospital it took thirty-two stitches to close the wound.

'I was put into a tiny room with four old people,' says Sean, 'and one died in the bed next to me. I heard the rattle and everything and I was truly terrified. But nothing has frightened me since.'

It is a measure of young Connery's resilience and single-mindedness of purpose that after five days in the hospital and another ten spent convalescing he returned home and within a week was out on The Meadows again with his sledge.

Neil Connery remembers his brother as the quiet one, physically strong but a loner more sensitive to atmosphere and surroundings than the rest of the family. However, he was no dreamer. On the contrary, he was a highly practical individual who, from a very early age, quickly cottoned on to the inescapable fact that without money there is no choice of action or freedom. And it wasn't too long before he decided to do something about it.

According to his mother, affectionately known as Effie, Tommy began earning at the age of eight when his brother was born. 'He delivered milk in the mornings and at night he helped out in a butcher's shop. He gave me every penny he earned and I banked it for him. When he left school he had £60 safely put away in his own account.'

He was no great scholar. At Darroch Secondary School English was the only subject he appeared to be good at and until he left just before he was fourteen years old he was up at 5 a.m. every morning of his young life to deliver milk as a part-time job, pushing a milk cart around the neighbourhood, darting up and down tenement stairs. When he left school he was taken on as a milk roundsman for the St Cuthbert's Co-operative Society. Out of bed at five every morning summer and winter he just had time for a breakfast of porridge and milk before clocking on at the depot where a fleet of horse-drawn milk floats would clatter out of St Cuthbert's at 5.30 a.m. sharp, racing each other to be the first over Dean Bridge.

After his milk round finished about three o'clock in the afternoon the boy would go home for a meal and then out again to deliver the evening newspapers covering two or three miles of the city streets on foot, a chore for which he received 5 shillings (now 25p) a week and which he counted as his own pocket money. His wage from the Co-op for a seven-day week was £2 14s. all of which he gave to his mother to help out with the housekeeping.

The days were long. After supper he would go to the stables to groom his horse, a pony inevitably named Tich because it was the smallest of the horses on the milk run. He developed a great affection for it and each night he would take his mother's brass polish to brighten the brasswork on its harness and the black lead she used for the grate to polish its hooves. Often he would stay there until nine or ten o'clock at night and once, when Tich was sick, he was there throughout the night feeding it with his own preparation, a mixture of turnip, bruised oats and cut hay which he boiled in treacle.

The care he lavished on Tich was amply repaid when, competing for the annual best horse and cart contest against a forty-strong opposition, he carried off a rosette for his pony and a Highly Commended award for himself. It was the first time in his life that he had ever won recognition for anything and he was both thrilled and excited. 'It was as though he'd won £100,' says his brother.

Every penny he could put by from his meagre earnings as a newspaper boy he saved, putting it in the Post Office Savings Bank. By the time he was sixteen he had more than £75 in his account. He thought of buying a motorbike but his father would have none of it. 'You're too young,' he told his son. So the boy went out and bought a piano instead. It was as though he wanted to see something tangible for his money and effort, regarding it as an investment, a visible piece of property owned.

The fact that no one in the family could play the piano seemed immaterial. It cost £56 10s. (£56.50) plus another £1 to have it delivered, and there it stood, a solid status symbol in the eyes of neighbours who expected music but heard instead only fragmented melodies of *Bluebells of Scotland* interspersed with *Annie Laurie* picked out with one uncertain finger.

His mother offered to pay for lessons but there were too many other distractions, such as football and the Sea Cadets which Connery had joined. He loved football because he was good at it. He had played centre-forward for his school team and then for a boys' club, Fetlor Amateurs, the year they won a cup in a newspaper competition. Later he played as a semi-professional for Bonyrigg Rose Athletic. Two scouts from East Fife, then a team in the Scottish First Division, watched him and sounded him out with a £25 signing fee. He turned them down because the idea of living away from home did not appeal to him then.

He was turned seventeen when he decided that there was a life outside Fountainbridge. A way of life that offered both security and independence. He joined the Royal Navy. His mother was not pleased. His father was resigned. 'If that's what you really want, son, then it's all right by me,' he said.

2
Body-Building

It was in Portsmouth that Tommy Connery acquired the tattoos that indelibly stamped him as a bona fide naval rating. They expressed the loyalties dearest to him: on the white of his right forearm worked in red and blue is the defiant motto SCOTLAND FOR EVER and below that the simple inscription MUM AND DAD. He wore them with pride.

From the outset Connery saw the Navy as an escape, believing it would open up new horizons. He had signed on for seven years' active service and another five on the reserve, but it didn't work out that way. Within two years he was invalided out with a duodenal ulcer.

The disability could have been a family weakness because both his father and his brother had ulcers or it may have had something to do with the excessive amounts of milk he drank as a child affecting his digestive system. His brother Neil describes his consumption in terms of gallons. Certainly of the eight pints his mother bought daily the boy drank four and then there were the additional pints that came by way of perks as a milk roundsman.

There was, however, another factor. What had not been taken into account were the tensions of service life on someone of Connery's temperament. He was a rugged individualist still uncertain of himself and where he was going and he did not easily conform to the service pattern. It was not the discipline in itself that worried him because that came all too easily to a boy who from the earliest years had disciplined himself to a gruelling schedule of work, often going to school and sitting there in sodden rain-wet clothes because he had had no time to go back home and change them. What really irked him about the Navy was the pecking order of its discipline whereby someone was always in a position of authority to tell him what to do – and with no come-back from him.

In one revealing moment he said: 'I don't like anyone telling me what to do. As a boy seaman there was an ordinary seaman telling me what to do. As an ordinary seaman there was an able seaman telling me what to do. As an able seaman . . . it was unending. Put it another way. I don't so much mind being told what to do provided I have respect for the person who is telling me, but there is nothing more boring, more annoying, more maddening than being told to do something by someone who is incompetent.'

So he had a few fights, took a few hidings before being invalided out and finding himself back in Fountainbridge on the threshold of twenty with very little to show for his naval service other than his tattoos, his ulcer, a diet sheet and a weekly disability pension of 6s 9d.

It was not the easiest time to look for work for someone with no academic qualifications or scholastic success. If the British Legion had not come to his rescue he would probably have emigrated.

They arranged for him to train as a French polisher and after the course he faced what looked like a permanent future in a dead-end job. He went to work for an undertaker. 'As soon as we knew the measurements of the latest customer I would start scraping and polishing his coffin. On a rush job I would stay there all night sometimes, sleeping in the coffin on which I was working. It can be comfortable enough provided you bring your own pillow – and it keeps your body firm.'

At this time he was concerned with building himself up because despite his height he was painfully lean. Through rigorous training his body was to become one of his most powerful assets. For the 15s. (75p) it cost him to join the Dunedin Amateur Weight-Lifting Club and a weekly subscription of 1s. 6d. (7½p) he devoted the evenings of Monday, Wednesday and Friday of each week to personal physical culture. He was not interested in competitive weight-lifting so much as in developing his physique to keep fit and look good for the girls.

The idea of body-building in Scotland was different from that in England where beefcake boys posed on podiums flexing their pectorals in an aura of baby oil. And Connery was contemptuous of men who would not even run for a bus in case they lost their bulk.

He bought himself a tracksuit, chest expanders and dumbbells to work out at home. Within a year his well-muscled body began to take on a streamlined shape, a broad-shouldered, symmetrical figure that he took to the Edinburgh School of Art where he hired himself out by the hour as a model. He says he could hold a pose for forty-five minutes standing in briefs holding a spear. And for 15s. (75p) per sitting he was in great demand. For a girls' painting class he was naked except for the barest essential, a posing pouch. He quit modelling he says because the girls always wanted to sketch close-ups and he feared to show his embarrassment.

Connery says he was introduced to sex at an early age playing doctors and nurses in the Edinburgh tenements. 'I was eight years old and it was a lurid introduction to sex but pretty basic. Although I can't remember a particular moment when I lost my virginity, it was a gradual acceptance that I no longer had it. I was never successful with ladies early on despite my knowledge. I was very shy.'

There was no fear of embarrassment when he was in control of the situation and he met girls at Binns Corner, the local lovers' traditional trysting place. If Tommy Connery worked hard he also played hard.

Once a week he would treat himself to a slap-up, blow-out dinner of steak and mushrooms rounded off with an ice-cream sundae at Ritchie's Restaurant. It cost him 10s. (50p) which was big money to him then but he felt his labours deserved it. And there were the Saturday night carousals with the boys at the Fountain Bar drinking with the likes of Billy Bird the electrician, Danny Fraser from the brewery and their mates who would bring a crate of beer and borrowed glasses to the Connery kitchen for a drinking party where they roared into song as Saturday night gave way to Sunday morning.

By now Connery was twenty-three and in that time he had had a variety of other jobs to the concern of his parents who wanted to see him settled in regular employment in a permanent trade. As a French polisher he had been employed, after his undertaking experience, by something like five cabinet makers in and around Edinburgh. He wasn't fired; he simply moved on for a bigger pay packet. For another couple of months he became a steelworker and then a cement-mixer, boosting his pay to around £15 a week with overtime. He insisted, despite her protests, on giving his mother more than she felt she needed or felt he could afford and so he moved on from job to job always looking for the right one at the right money. He was determined not to work for what he called 'sweeties' as his father, for whom he had both love and respect, had been forced to do.

It was his father who had taught him to swim when he was only five years old and now he was a powerful enough swimmer to be taken on as a lifeguard at the Portobello pool on Edinburgh's outskirts. He was a natural for this job because from the time his father plunged him in at the deep end on their first visit to the swimming baths he showed he had no fear.

So far as this five-year-old was concerned the three-foot shallow end of the bath was for kids and he learned to swim by taking a running jump into the six-foot end where his father dog-paddled alongside him to ensure he came to no harm. His father need not have worried. The boy was like a fish in water and when he took on the job as a lifeguard he saved at least one woman from drowning when the artificial wave unit came on and she was clearly in difficulties. He took the job, as he did every job he had, seriously and he was not amused when his younger brother Neil turned up at the pool one day and by way of a prank started splashing and threshing around in the middle shouting 'Help! Save me! Help!' Tommy was halfway out of his sweater ready to dive in when he saw it was Neil with an impish grin on his face. Tommy turned away and his voice was curt. 'Drown,' he said.

By now Connery had the body and the build to take on another job to supplement his earnings. He became a bouncer in an Edinburgh night club where the bands of Sandy Brown, Alex Welsh and Al Fairweather played trad jazz. There were no reports of any trouble from the clientele who, having surveyed the size and shape of the bouncer, appeared to take an even deeper interest in the music and musicians. It was Connery's first tenuous connection with showbusiness of any kind.

He had brief but closer contact with the theatre when Anna Neagle arrived in Edinburgh with a show called *Sixty Glorious Years*. In answer to an advertisement he landed himself with a part as a walk-on but only because they needed six soldiers over six feet tall. He had to travel to London before he finally knew, with certainty, what he wanted to do with his life.

He was working for the *Edinburgh Evening News* cleaning the machine-room equipment when Archie Brennan, a former Mr Scotland and a member of the Dunedin Weight-Lifting Club suggested that he entered for the Mr Universe contest which was being held at the Scala Theatre near London's Tottenham Court Road. He was interested. He took time off from work and rode down to London on his motorbike, which he had acquired after leaving the Navy. It had proved invaluable as transport to his various jobs in and around Edinburgh. By contrast the journey to London seemed like a marathon. It took nine hours and it was a somewhat saddlesore young man who arrived in the capital to face the judges. Nevertheless he made his impact.

He was selected as a runner-up in his class and awarded a small bronze medallion. It was some consolation prize for his time and effort, but the best was yet to come. He was told that actors were being auditioned for parts in the hit musical *South Pacific* which was running at the Theatre Royal, Drury Lane. He could not sing or dance but that seemed to him no problem. What he was after was the job. When he arrived he discovered they were looking for chorus boys for a touring version.

In the darkened auditorium they asked him if he was an actor. He said he was. They asked if he could sing. He said he could. They gave him a script and asked him to read it. He fumbled and dropped some pages, watching the loose leaves flutter about the stage. They were not impressed.

'Hurry up,' they said. 'We haven't got all day.'

'Neither have I,' he replied. He tossed what was left of the script into the air and started to walk away.

The director in charge called out: 'Hey, bring that guy back here.' When he returned he was asked whether his shoulders were all his own. Told they were he was given a script again and asked to read from it in an American accent. How he managed he is not quite sure but they took another look at his shoulders and said: 'Okay, mister. You've got yourself a part in *South Pacific*.'

He asked: 'How much do I get?'

There was a startled silence. Everyone looked at the American producer sitting comfortably in the stalls who simply said: 'It doesn't concern me.'

The young Connery retorted: 'But it concerns *me*.' It was with some surprise that they found themselves discussing his salary of £12 a week.

This was the turning point. His family say he was ecstatic when he returned to Edinburgh with the news. He burst in on them shouting,

'I've got it! I've got it! I've got a part in *South Pacific*!' According to his mother he practised dance steps like a man demented for the next forty-eight hours. And he told his brother: 'This is the start. This is what I've been looking for. It's what I've always wanted, Neil.'

The show moved round the country and he travelled from town to town with it on his motorbike, loving every nomadic minute of it. On the first night on tour in Bristol they had just got to the bit about Washing That Man Right Out of My Hair when the leading man suddenly turned grey and said he could not go on.

'He was not at all well,' says Connery now, 'and everyone thought he would keel over. So they dropped the next set immediately – and it fell on top of me.'

During the course of the tour he graduated from chorus boy to a small part by the time it reached the King's Theatre in Edinburgh and when it returned there a second time several months later he was in a featured role as Lieutenant Buzz Adams.

Tommy Connery had ceased to exist. The name on the programme read: Sean Connery.

3
Star in the Making

In London's fashionable Abbey Road, long before the Beatles came on the scene and immortalized it in song, Peter Noble, showbusiness journalist and film buff, was hopefully seeking a baby-sitter. Whoever he may have had in mind as a suitable applicant most certainly did not include the broad-shouldered 6ft 2in. Scotsman who came to his door and introduced himself as Sean Connery.

'He was a bit hard up at the time,' says Peter, 'and for ten bob he agreed to look after the baby. If he had to change a nappy he got another ten bob and there were times when we'd come back from some film function or other and he'd say, "I had to change a nappy twice tonight," so he got thirty bob. He was going through a fairly tough patch then, but we became friends and later when he didn't need the money he would come round and mow the lawn or sit for us while watching television. He was a good handyman and often he would bring a bottle of Scotch along. Actually we got to know him through the Gardners who lived just up the road.'

The Gardners, journalist Llew Gardner now with Thames Television and his wife Merry Archard, lived in a first-floor flat in Brondesbury Villas, Kilburn, the unfashionable end of Abbey Road, and they had a room to let. At that time Merry Archard was working on a women's magazine with Julie Hamilton, a photographer whose mother is Jill Craigie, then as now married to Michael Foot, the Labour leader.

Julie, a tall and blue-eyed blonde with shapely legs and an engaging, attractive smile, had become enamoured of an unknown actor whom she had met on her travels. His name was Sean Connery and he was looking for somewhere to live. For 12s. 6d. (62½p) a week he took the room and became the Gardners' lodger for almost a year.

'My first impressions were of a very large, very hirsute Scottish young man who kept working out with dumbbells,' says Llew Gardner. 'I remember going to his room once and he asked me if I'd mind moving some of the weights – those disc things on the end. It was all I could do to roll them along the floor, let alone pick them up. He had a collection of pictures showing himself in body beautiful poses for which he must have shaved all over because there wasn't a trace of hair to be seen. What struck me most about him was that he was a very canny Scot not easily impressed by those in a position to offer him money and fame.

'He was a great bargainer. He bought a pair of corduroys in the Kilburn market and was delighted not so much with the trousers as his ability to beat down the street trader to a price he was prepared to pay. He could – and did – go out and buy the cheapest piece of meat and turn out a very good stew. To me it was extraordinary, not so much that it was done well, but that it was done at all.

'A similar thing happened when he and Julie went out to buy a large double bed. Second-hand, of course. He got it at the price he wanted which was probably because it had only three legs.

'It so happened that I owned thirteen volumes of the collected works of Stalin for which I had very little use. Apart from anything else it was such unrewarding prose. Anyhow, we thought it would be put to more practical use by becoming the fourth leg of the bed. I imagine it was the first time Stalin had ever been screwed that way.'

If Sean Connery was making love on top of Stalin by night he was ploughing through Proust by day, all twelve volumes of him. And not only Proust but Shakespeare and Ibsen and James Joyce as well, to name but a few. Connery had taken the advice of a man called Robert Henderson, an actor and director, who had mapped out a course of reading for this would-be actor with no training or apprenticeship for his craft. It was a course that would have daunted a public or grammar school boy let alone someone who had survived just the barest formal education.

During the run of *South Pacific* he had been made to feel inferior in intellect by Southerners who had either been to stage school or who had benefited from higher schooling. When they had discussions they had talked of books, plays, ideas, of which he knew nothing. 'I got a list of books and it took me eighteen months to work my way through them including Thomas Wolfe, *War and Peace* and Stanislavsky on dramatic theory.'

Self-education was one thing. Finding the right work was another. At Twentieth-Century Fox he lost a part in *Boy on a Dolphin* because he was too tall. At Rank he missed out on *High Tide at Noon* because he was too dark. His problem was, as another studio told him, that he was 'too different'. At the Old Vic, Michael Bentall dismissed him gently with: 'You don't fit into the composition here. Take elocution lessons. Study your diction.'

'He worked hard at it,' says Llew Gardner. 'He took elocution lessons and it showed. There were nights at home when we sat around reading poetry, particularly Burns. I remember Sean's version of *Scots Wha Hae*. He recited it in a dramatic conversational whisper as though confiding to comrades around a camp fire. Most declaim those lines telling of where Wallace bled in sonorous tones but his whispered version was an interpretation of his own and very effective.'

Julie Hamilton introduced him to her mother and her stepfather who also had a house in Abbey Road, but at the more fashionable end. He and Michael Foot, whom he admired as a politician, got along well enough discussing literature and politics, but Jill Craigie was dubious about this young man. With a mother's eye she saw a penniless young actor with no future on whom her daughter had a considerable crush. She was unaware at this time of just how close a relationship they enjoyed, but according to Llew Gardner Julie was under great pressure from home to break with this wild, ne'er-do-well actor who showed no signs of getting anywhere.

According to Neil Connery, although his brother had been a good saver, keeping money aside for a rainy day, he had one spell out of work when all he had coming in was unemployment benefit and his weekly outgoings in meals, lodgings, fares and elocution lessons were totalling £10 a week. He cut out his fares by buying a rusty old bicycle for a few shillings and kept it chained outside his lodgings. It was a lady's bike but no one made any jokes about that when they saw who was riding it.

It was around this period that Sean's mother Effie had a visitor in Edinburgh, an Indian salesman wearing a turban who came to her door with an array of silks over his arm. She was particularly taken by a blue and gold bedspread and he suggested that if he could sell it to her he would tell her fortune.

After some hard bargaining (like her son she seemed to know the value of an article right down to the bottom line) she bought it and he said: 'Now I'll tell your fortune, lady.' She refused.

'Go away with you,' she said, trying to shut the door.

He insisted. Taking her hand he peered at her palm and said: 'I see you have a son, lady. No, two sons. Two big, strong, handsome sons. One day one of your sons will be a very famous man. Very, very famous.'

'That'll be the day,' Sean's mother said. And closed the door.

In London Sean Connery was coming to the end of what he calls his Too Period. This was the time when no matter what work he went after they told him he was either too tall or too big, too Scottish or too Irish, or too young or too old for the part directors had in mind. Had he consulted an astrologer he need not have worried. According to one his chart would have read: 'You are honest and just, generous, affectionate, far-sighted and have good judgment. You love music and have considerable talent for it. You are an amusing and interesting talker; humorous and good company. You love your home and are solicitous for the happiness of your family and loved ones. You have the characteristics of a leader. You are sincere and demonstrative in your love and bitter in your hatred. Pick a congenial mate and you will be very happy. You will also be lucky.'

After the two years he had spent touring in *South Pacific* he had managed to sustain himself with a number of straight roles in repertory, notably at the Q Theatre, which led to television work: Jack Benny had him playing the part of a tough Italian porter in the *Jack Benny Show* for B.B.C.; Lorne Greene drafted him as a tough smuggler in his *Sailor of Fortune* series on I.T.V.; and he appeared in a *Dixon of Dock Green*. There were also parts in unmemorable films such as *Hell Drivers*, *No Road Back*, *Time Lock* and *Action of the Tiger* with Van Johnson and Martine Carol. In this he had to pounce on Martine with uncontrolled passion. Reportedly, she took one look at his virile torso and murmured, 'Am I supposed to run away from that?'

Hailed as rugged and tough, he had played a lorry driver in *Hell Drivers* and a welder in *Time Lock* and might well have spent the rest of his screen career cast as a bricklayer or road digger had it not been for an actor called Jack Palance and a man called Bob Goldstein, then head of Twentieth-Century Fox production in England.

The B.B.C. had wanted Palance to play the part of the battered

prizefighter in Rod Serling's *Requiem for a Heavyweight*, the role
he had played in the American production. Because of a film
commitment in Hollywood Palace had had to cry off and the
search was on for an actor to portray Mountain McClintock, the
punch-drunk heavyweight has-been. Alvin Rakoff, the Canadian-
born television producer who had been a Toronto amateur
lightweight in his day, tested nearly forty six-footers for the part,
including ex-professional fighters and amateur boxers. It was not
until Sean Connery weighed in at 13st. 8lbs and read the part that
Rakoff found his star in the making.

On 31 March 1957 *Requiem for a Heavyweight* went out on
B.B.C. television as the Sunday night play – and the phones did not
stop ringing. Everywhere there was praise for what was a
remarkable achievement. One critic called it 'a shattering
performance' and up in Fountainbridge where he watched it Sean's
father was moved to say, 'By heaven that was smashing.' Bob
Goldstein of Twentieth-Century Fox picked up a phone and called
Hollywood, convinced Connery would be a world star. The Rank
Organization wanted to sign him to a long-term contract.

'I must have received 200 offers the next day,' Connery says. 'I
think I had every casting director in London knocking on my door.
It was quite a part considering I had to talk through a gum-shield for
ninety minutes. And all for £35!'

To escape the pressures he and Julie Hamilton drove north to
Scotland in her sports car for a week's holiday in order to sort out •
the various offers and assess his chances.

'What really impressed me,' says Llew Gardner, 'was his absolute
cool-headedness when weighing up the offers. Here was a young
man being offered contracts that in the eyes of most struggling
actors would look like three lemons in the window of a one-armed
bandit and treating them as though any well-muscled, weight-lifting
ex-milkman from Scotland could expect no less.'

Sean Connery finally settled with Twentieth-Century Fox for a
seven-year contract but because of the quality of the films in which
he was involved it did not quite work out the way he hoped. Neither
did his year-long affair with Julie Hamilton.

When Sean Connery returned to London it was to a bachelor pad
he had acquired in St John's Wood, a studio flat above a couple of
garages of Wavell Mews. There he entertained and cooked for a
number of girlfriends and acquaintances including a highly

intelligent blonde actress whom he had met for the first time in a television studio that year when they were involved in a production of *Anna Christie*. Her name was Diane Cilento. She would later say that she felt their romance was clinched when he bought her Vespa scooter.

4
Hollywood

Sean Connery was in Hollywood in April 1958 when the phone rang in his hotel room. A voice, low-pitched and serious, sounded in his ear and the line it uttered could have come straight from a Hollywood script for a 'B' movie. 'You'd better get out of town,' the voice said.

In other circumstances it would have been laughable; a hoax maybe. But Sean Connery knew enough to understand that this was no friend playing some kind of joke but a warning meant to be taken seriously.

The day before, Lana Turner's fourteen-year-old daughter Cheryl Crane had murdered one Johnny Stompanato, a gangster with a playboy image who was her mother's lover. Outside the film star's bedroom door the girl had attacked him with a carving knife and stabbed him to death.

According to Sean Connery's telephone caller Lana had mentioned him in some of the letters she had written to Stompanato from London while she and the leading man of her choice were making *Another Time, Another Place*. Understandable enough, but in the case of a man such as Johnny Stompanato somewhat indiscreet.

Indeed, it was a highly suspicious Stompanato who had followed Lana Turner to Britain the previous October where the Joe Kaufman production in which she was involved with Sean Connery (in the film they were having an affair) was bedevilled by problems. When Stompanato arrived it was to discover most of the cast stricken by Asian flu.

Lana was languishing in bed in a Belgravia flat for which the studio was paying £75 a week when he flew in.

'What's a star like you doing in a dump like this?' he stormed. 'It's a pigsty.'

He called in Harley Street specialists, nurses and maids and when she was well enough he moved her to The White Lodge, a house that belonged to actress Zoe Gail in Hampstead's 'Millionaires' Row'. The rent was then £100 a week but when Stompanato arrived the bills began soaring into hundreds of pounds. The studio was paying its star £150 a week to cover expenses but the expenses far exceeded this with the helping hand of Mr Stompanato.

He went to the studios. Quiet and menacing he sat in the shadows on Stage Three at Elstree Studios looking like the sort of minder you see at the dimly-lit manager's table of some frowsy nightclub. No one talked to him at first but he was made to understand his presence was not helping the production. Quarrels followed at the Hampstead house. According to the German housekeeper Rosa Merk, Stompanato threatened to break every bone in the star's body. He was a big man with a temper to match and many times Lana Turner telephoned from the studio saying she was too frightened to return home.

There was a final scene at The White Lodge when Lana and the housekeeper were alone there. When Stompanato came in, Lana ran to her room and locked the door. Soon afterwards two Scotland Yard men raced to the house. Inside they found doors shattered, swinging on their hinges, and Stompanato ran out into the arms of detectives. He left quickly for the States having been warned by Scotland Yard to leave the country.

This was the background to the warning given to Sean Connery who, under the terms of his seven-year contract with Twentieth-Century Fox, had been loaned out to Paramount to make *Another Time, Another Place*.

Now, in Hollywood, Sean was being told by his friendly phone caller that 'an associate' of the suddenly late and very dead Mr Stompanato was out looking for him. And it did not need much imagination to conjure up a portrait of the kind of character who would be an associate of a man who was a known thug, a henchman of top gangster Bugsy Siegel and a bodyguard of the even more infamous Mickey Cohen.

Sean was six feet two inches tall and around 180 lbs of solid muscle, sinew and bone at the time but he had his priorities.

'My problem,' Sean says, 'was that I owed my hotel $600 and I was right in the middle of a big row with the studio. But I got out and went to a motel in the San Fernando Valley where I lay low.

Nothing did happen, but it was scary as hell for a while.'

Sean Connery had gone to Hollywood to make *Darby O'Gill and the Little People* with Janet Munro. Hollywood's recognition of his potential, however badly handled, had its effect. With luck, talent and a disregard for the conventions of the day he had built a career without background, without influence and without hypocrisy. Now, with an assured income and a foreseeable future he had begun to get the big star build-up which meant voice production, singing lessons, interviews, invitations to premieres, parties and spots to be seen.

Lana Turner had picked him from screen tests of a number of young hopefuls sent back to Hollywood by the producer and director of *Another Time, Another Place*. They had been scouting England for a new face to play opposite their 38-year-old star and on the verge of twenty-eight he suddenly found himself sandwiched between America's original sweater girl and Britain's Glynis Johns, two ladies who between them shared seventy years and seven husbands. 'In the film I was supposedly married to Glynis but I was also having an affair with Lana and I died halfway through. It was only when I was asked what it was like to make love to an older woman that for the first time in my life I became aware of a woman's age.'

He also became aware of the penalties attached to being a studio property. As Lana Turner, who wore a figure-hugging black dress for their first introductory candlelit dinner together in England said: 'The movies have given me a great deal and the only thing I regret is a loss of privacy. When you have deep hurts and anguishes you may not want your own family to know about them. But if you are a star they are splashed over every newspaper for the world to see. But I suppose everything has its price.'

It was a price that Sean Connery determined he would not pay.

To Patricia Lewis, a newspaper columnist who had invited him to lunch for the purpose of interviewing this latest discovery who was being boosted by the film machine as Britain's answer to Brando, he cited the case of Jayne Mansfield.

'Even London wasn't big enough to lose her,' he said. 'She moved everywhere with a great entourage in the spotlight all the time. There's a difference between being dedicated and desiccated. Stars can get so submerged by success they can't lift a tissue to wipe their nose without someone there to help.'

And with that he rode off, an incongruously large and powerful figure on his small sea-green Vespa scooter, leaving Patricia Lewis with the impression that success meant not only the freedom to blow his own nose, but the freedom to do so without it being made a matter of public concern.

He knew he was not in a position yet to select what he would or would not do, but he was also aware that the Lana Turner picture meant he would be a recognized figure in America when he started working there. He was therefore prepared to endure certain frustrations provided they furthered his career.

'I think Sean always knew where he was going,' says Llew Gardner, 'and how he was going to get there. For example, Hollywood had this thing about his hair. It was receding rapidly for a young man but it was hereditary and he couldn't do much about it. But they sent him off to various clinics and trichologists.

'He went happily enough but it was all to no avail. He had more hair on his back and shoulders than on his scalp but it didn't seem to worry him at all. I remember he went through one course of treatment at a famous clinic. They asked him: "What shampoo do you use?" and he said: "What's shampoo?" If that sounds naive you must remember he was a man without any vanity. There was nothing naive about him when it came to business. After offers of contracts in Hollywood he had insisted on clauses whereby if they did not do certain things in a certain period of time they would bring him back to England.'

Sean Connery was away in Hollywood for about six months and when he returned he was, according to his former friends, a changed man in his attitudes. He had broken up with Julie Hamilton and he no longer went out playing football or to the pubs where fellow Scots and a few kindred spirits such as Ronnie Fraser and Ian McNaughton and Llew Gardner had been wont to meet and swap stories.

Whether this new Connery had something to do with Diane Cilento's influence they did not know, but they suspected it.

'After Diane came into his life things were never the same again,' says Peter Noble. 'He seemed to have cut himself off. Of course we've met since over the years and we'll exchange a word or two of greeting but the old relationship is no longer there.

'He entertained a number of ladies in his flat. I know Lana Turner went there. But I think it was Diane who really fascinated him.'

Llew Gardner says: 'It's true some of his friends felt he had dropped them. From the time he became reasonably well known everyone was aware there was a different situation colouring their relationships. I do think it was a deliberate policy on his part. It was as though he knew he was changing both as a person and as an actor and therefore new patterns of behaviour, new lifestyles were required. He had a very shrewd idea of what he wanted to do. When he came back from the States he went into the theatre seriously and it showed great independence of mind when he got out of his Hollywood contract.'

Apart from the film *The Longest Day* in which he played a small but effective part, Sean Connery now concentrated on dedicating himself to his craft, working in the theatre and on television where he received almost uniformly solid praise from the critics. Both he and Diane Cilento attended movement classes, which they felt to be an essential if not vital ingredient of their acting equipment. In Sean they helped to develop his panther-like walk that would become markedly famous.

They seemed to be good for one another. If Diane was instrumental in helping to alienate him from his London coterie of friends, and she had a distinct antipathy for journalists in particular, she endeared herself to his family. According to Neil Connery the first time Sean brought her to their home in Fountainbridge 'she plopped down in a chair, kicked off her shoes, and acted as though she had lived there all her life'.

Diane Cilento came from a town called Mooloolaba in Queensland, Australia, but her surname was taken from the Italian town Cilento from which her paternal grandfather was exiled because he was a follower of the Italian patriot Garibaldi. She left Australia at the age of fourteen to go to America with her father, Sir Raphael Cilento, a doctor who worked for the World Health Organization.

It was an enforced trip. 'I was always in trouble at boarding school in Australia. One day I went out to a telephone box and rang the headmistress. Imitating my mother's voice I said: "Will it be all right if I invite Diane and some of her friends for the weekend?" The headmistress said it would and I couldn't resist adding: "And how is my little D getting on?" I knew I'd been a perfect pest but the headmistress replied, "Oh, wonderfully well!" So I took my friends out for a grand, mad weekend and felt a lot better for it.

'The trouble came three months later when a teacher spotted a diary on a friend's desk. In it she had set out the entire escapade – and I was expelled.'

At sixteen she left America for England and enrolled at R.A.D.A. before serving her apprenticeship as an actress with the Manchester Repertory Company which she found 'grey, foggy and cultural'. And at eighteen she married an Italian writer, Andrea Volpe, by whom she had a daughter, but the marriage was not working out.

The first night she met Sean Connery's parents she stayed up talking with them until two o'clock in the morning and Mrs Connery, fascinated by her accent and stories, called her 'a wee smasher'. In Scotland praise came no higher.

5

Sean Connery is James Bond

At their London headquarters in Mayfair's South Audley Street, film producers Harry Saltzman and Albert R. Broccoli, who is known to intimates in the business as 'Cubby', were awaiting the arrival of the man they had been told could breathe life into the fictional James Bond on screen. With them was a man called Stanley Sopel, an accountant by profession, who was billed as assistant producer.

Harry and Cubby had a deal to make a Bond picture. For this immediate purpose they needed a shell company that could be used in a hurry and from some dusty shelf had plucked one called Eon. No one knew what the letters stood for but if, as they suspected, the acronym meant something like eternity they knew they could not afford to wait that long.

The film rights to the first Bond book *Casino Royale* had been sold by Ian Fleming's agent Robert Fenn to Gregory Ratoff, the Russian-American director and actor who had been fascinated by the gambling techniques which took up half the book, but Harry and Cubby were not interested in *Casino Royale*. They chose *Dr No* as their first picture and they paid for the rights on the nose with options to film anything Fleming had written since or would write in the future. Cubby then made a deal with United Artists whereby twelve months after the release of the first Bond picture they could pick up the second with options for future ones.

Deals are the kiss of life to Cubby Broccoli. He is the product of an Italian-American family who ran a truck farm outside New York ferrying vegetables (including the broccoli one of his uncles introduced to the U.S.A.) for sale in that city. It is an odd coincidence that Cubby, like Sean Connery, once flirted briefly with the business of making coffins. That was when he left the family firm to become manager of the United Casket Company but found it all too morbid to contemplate. He went to Hollywood where he sold jewellery and then cosmetics until he found a job in the mailroom at Twentieth-Century Fox and worked his way up to become assistant to the legendary director Howard Hawks. His next move was to set himself up as an agent with clients such as Lana Turner and Ava Gardner to brighten his day and his bank balance. He arrived in Britain in 1950 attracted by the incentive of Easy money, a government subsidy for home-produced movies, and formed Warwick Films with a fellow American Irving Allen. Aided by the kickback, they made what Cubby described as 'profitable crap' but now, in 1961, his intuition and instinct told him he was about to tap a goldmine.

United Artists had put a ceiling of $1 million on the production of *Dr No* and the first questions were: who plays the lead? who directs? Among directors' names suggested were Ken Annakin, Guy Hamilton, Ken Hughes, but it was with Terence Young, who had worked with Cubby in Warwick days, that they made a deal. Now all attention was on who would play Jimmy the Bond.

According to Stanley Sopel, the first person to suggest Sean Connery for the role of Bond was Patricia Lewis, the columnist who had interviewed him in his first flush of fame four years earlier. She was now working for the *Daily Express* which was serializing the Bond thrillers and had an obvious interest in the filming of *Dr No*. Indeed, the newspaper had decided to run a poll inviting readers to choose their own Bond for the screen and from a field of ten runners Sean Connery emerged among the top three. His television performances in plays such as Arthur Miller's *The Crucible*, *The Pets*, in which he co-starred with Robert Shaw, and *Boy With the Meat Axe* had given him quite a following.

'Patricia had talked to Sean over dinner with the producer Ben Fisz,' says Sopel, 'and I think she saw him as a potential Gary Cooper, someone who could be an international star. Anyway it was she who introduced him to us as a possible Bond and I could hardly believe my eyes the first time I saw him. I was looking for Fleming's sophisticated Commander James Bond R.N. when through the door came the most appallingly dressed young man I'd ever seen in my life. He looked as though he'd just come in off the street to ask for the price of a cup of tea.'

It is true that when Connery arrived for his first meeting with the film-makers he looked about as far removed from Fleming's prescription for an impeccably tailored 007 with sophisticated tastes as it is possible to get. Cubby Broccoli says: 'He was rough and tough and didn't have the right clothes. He was wearing baggy, unpressed trousers, a brown shirt without a tie and suede shoes and he thumped and pounded the desk and told us what he wanted. I think that's what impressed us: the fact that he'd got balls.'

From the beginning Connery had decided to play it tough and cool. He refused to test for the part. 'You either take me as I am or not at all,' he said in his flat Scottish burr. 'You'll have to back your own judgment.'

When he left the office the producers brooded over what they called his 'dark, cruel good looks' and, unknown to him as he left the building, peered from a window watching his retreating back. And there was something about his gait, the way he moved his athletic body that finally decided them.

'We saw him bounce across the street like he was Superman,' Cubby confides, 'and Harry and I believed we had to go along with him no matter what anyone else said.'

So it was not so much the interview, more the benefit of the movement classes he had attended with Diane Cilento that clinched the role for Sean Connery. He had all the threatening grace and power of a panther on the prowl, one of the essential physical attributes that made the girls so available and, if necessary, disposable in the deadly embrace of Fleming's hero.

'The difference between him and other young actors was like the difference between a still photograph and a film,' says Broccoli. 'When Connery started to move he came alive.'

Ever mindful of the value of publicity, however, Harry and Cubby felt they should test at least eight or ten actors for the part and the likely candidates were duly lined up at Twickenham studios. Sean Connery was not among them. 'How could I get over in a few moments the comedy I knew to be essential? I knew the thing couldn't be taken seriously and later I got the script worked round that way.'

A week later Sean Connery had a contract negotiated with his agent Richard Hatton. And the message went out: Sean Connery *is* James Bond. His fee for that first Bond picture has been put at various figures ranging from £3,000 to £15,000, but according to Stanley Sopel Connery's fee for ten weeks' work was £25,000.

'I should know,' he says, 'because part of my duty was to restrict his spending. Sean would come to me for money to meet his running expenses. "But you had £25 on Tuesday," I'd say. "Today's only Friday. Take it easy."'

The first task facing the film-makers was to transform this man who appeared somewhat gauche when it came to the social graces into a credible Bond. He was sufficient in size with a powerful frame to match but apart from that there was nothing to suggest the lifestyle of Fleming's fictional hero. James Bond had a Savile Row wardrobe, made-to-measure shirts, club memberships, knowledgeable tastes in food and wine. Connery had one off-the-peg suit and the odd sports jacket and was an informal drinker of beer and Scotch whisky who wasn't interested in martinis shaken or stirred, much less Bond's meticulously elaborate dry martini 'served in a deep champagne goblet, three measures of Gordon's, one of vodka, half a measure of Kina Lillet'.

Indeed, when Ian Fleming met Sean Connery for the first time he confided his misgivings to Sopel. 'I was looking for Commander James Bond, not an overgrown glorified stunt man,' he said.

Fleming was to revise this instant assessment when he saw Connery bring his own interpretation to the role, suggesting that the actor was a shrewd choice, 'not quite what I had in mind in the beginning, but he would be if I wrote the books over again'.

Connery says: 'I had to start playing Bond from scratch – not even Ian Fleming knew much about Bond at this time.'

He was right. Fleming always insisted he had never intended Bond to be a character, merely a peg on which to hang a story. 'It is other people who have put their own overcoats on him and build him into what they admire.'

It is why one wonders how much of Fleming was in Bond. He once said: 'People connect me simply because I happen to like scrambled eggs and short-sleeved shirts and some of the things he does, like gambling, but I certainly haven't got his guts nor his very lively appetite. It's all pillow fantasy stuff. Bang-bang. Kiss-kiss. The sort of thing you'd expect from an adolescent mind, which I happen to possess. As a matter of fact, I don't particularly like Bond which is why I didn't set him down as a particularly likeable fellow. All that fuss about his speckled eggs being boiled $3^{2}/_{3}$ of a minute. The proper time for a boiled egg is $3^{1}/_{2}$ minutes, the way I take mine.'

The way Sean Connery took his egg, in private of course, was the way he had been shown as a boy. He simply pierced a hole in the shell and sucked out the raw contents.

'It was Terence Young who groomed Sean Connery for the role of James Bond,' Sopel says. 'Terence Young is the perfect English gentleman even if he is Irish.' He laughs. What Sopel was talking about was the kitting out of Connery with the outward trappings of success allied to a privileged background; a veneer that could be worn like light armour. And Sean Connery went along with it not because he liked it or had any cravings to be a part of it but because it helped him to flesh out the character. As for the rest, it was like going to the wardrobe department. Besides, the underprivileged Scot had already made up his mind how he was going to play this upper-middle-class English agent: tongue-in-cheek. As Terence Young says: 'Sean is the only man I know who hasn't been changed by material success — and that's something I can't even say about myself.'

Terence Young, born in Shanghai, educated at Harrow, a Cambridge Blue and former Guards officer who had been a tank commander in the Second World War, had worked with Sean before. He had directed him in a film called *Action of the Tiger* and confesses: 'I mucked up that film. Connery came to me and said in that very Scots accent of his: "Sir, am I going to be a success in this?" I said, "No, but keep on swimming. Just keep at it and I'll make it up to you."'

And he did make it up to him with that first Bond film. In terms of tailored clothes, barbers who prided themselves on being tonsorial artists, choosing the best wines and eating the finest food it would be difficult to fault Terence Young's knowledge and experience. He is probably one of the few men in the world who wears a silk handkerchief in the pocket of a short-sleeved shirt, and he is, according to his wife, 'a perfectionist in everything'.

Sean Connery acknowledges drily: 'Terence has always been a sharp dresser. I should think that even when he was broke he dressed well. I like dressing well enough but the real flair is Terence's. He adores all that.'

He operated with style and panache, introducing the screen's first 007 to the intimacies of the clubs of St James's and the restaurants of Mayfair that mattered, and to a tailor, one Anthony Sinclair, who entered into the spirit of the exercise by rising at 0700 hours to operate from an exclusive salon in Conduit Street where he was generally acknowledged to be a Savile Row classicist for the top people in the business. He considered Connery had the perfect figure for a tailor to demonstrate his skills. 'He is a dream for a tailor,' he told me. 'His legs are marvellous and as for his figure, it is athletic with a 33-inch waist, a 46-inch chest and a nice firm 42 around the seat.'

Those who wondered how Mr Sinclair would manage a smooth and unobtrusive line to hide the Beretta that Agent 007 would carry in a shoulder-holster under his armpit underestimated his ingenuity. Not for nothing was he once voted Tailor of the Year. He took great pride in his craft from the paper pattern stage to the delivered work of art, all of which he could do himself. When challenged he said: 'When you have fitted a famous magician such as Channing Pollock with full evening dress to hide all those damn doves he carries about him for his act you may say that Mr Connery's armpit holds no fears for me.'

Once on the set Sean Connery always obeyed the cardinal rule of turning up on time. It was this professionalism that endeared him to the camera crews.

His co-operation with stunt men was freely acknowledged. Bob Simmons who was his stunt man says Connery was always a joy to work with because his reactions were those of a natural athlete with an added dimension. 'He knew how to make a scene look good for the cameras which is much more difficult than it looks.'

It is hardly surprising, with all this going for him, that *Dr No* established Sean Connery as James Bond with the boldness of an Identikit picture. There was the playboy image, the commando-style constitution, the impeccably tailored figure that made a tall target for assassins, and the sceptical eyebrows which radiated more sex appeal than Fleming's original concept of Bond's prep school comma of black hair. The Scottish burr, much less pronounced than in real life, wiped out any suggestion of class and his nonchalance in death-trapped situations was tinged with savoir-faire.

'It would be a shame to waste that Dom Perignon by hitting me with it,' purrs Dr No.

'Really?' retorts Bond. 'I prefer the '53 myself.'

Connery says he knew *Dr No* had all the ingredients of a hit. 'I just sat tight and waited.'

He did not have to wait long. The film made its money back on the London run alone. It was hardly surprising in retrospect. Apart from the initial impact of Connery, Bond addicts have never forgotten their first glimpse of his soul-mate Honey Rider, the original 007 girl Ursula Andress, breasting the surf and striding out along that creamy Jamaican beach, a dagger strapped to the belt of her wet, white bikini. Almost from the first reel, James Bond's sexual drive and male vanity were constantly satisfied by an almost endless supply of beautiful girls, but Ursula Andress, Swiss-born with her exquisitely-timed movement, was the first. The original blueprint and still, for many, the best of a list that was to become lusciously and lasciviously long.

So they not only envied Sean Connery as James Bond. Through the image he portrayed on the screen he acted out the common man's fantasies, and with some of the world's most beautiful women.

When publicity men seized on the catch-line 'Sean Connery *is* James Bond', everybody began to believe it. Except Sean Connery himself. A practical man, he had no time for illusion when the day's work was done. Like a carpenter, a bricklayer or a lorry driver he considered that when he clocked off he had a private life that belonged to him and which he should be able to enjoy.

In the States *Dr No* was not an overwhelming box-office hit. Not at first. One exhibitor said: 'I can't sell this Limey detective to our people in the South.' Exactly one year later the man was the highest bidder for the privilege of showing the second Bond film, *From Russia With Love*. That picture launched the Bond phenomenon in America.

6

Marriage on the Rock

It is doubtful whether marriage was on Sean Connery's mind when he left his London mews home on a cold January morning in 1962 bound for Jamaica and the location scenes for *Dr No*. On an icy patch outside his garage he slipped and twisted his knee. It caused him some pain and the nagging discomfort was not eased until he came back to Britain in April and had an operation to remove the cartilage.

'I'm not planning to get married,' he said from his hospital bed, 'although there's always some girl trying to move in on me. It's getting rid of them that's the problem.'

Nevertheless, his days as a bachelor appeared to be numbered because a few weeks later he was in the market looking for a house. A house, moreover, big enough for a family.

'Sean,' says Denis Selinger who was his agent at one time, 'is secretive. He always liked the ladies and being a very good-looking virile man I imagine they presented no problem.'

Sean Connery has always been secretive about his girlfriends, ever since he was sixteen and his father answered the door to two of them who called for him one night at his Edinburgh home.

'Is Tammy coming out?' they asked.

'Not tonight,' his father said with a grin. 'His mother's giving him his bath.' The girls fled giggling down the stairs. Sean, who had overheard his father at the door, was angry.

'Fancy telling them that,' he said. 'What will they think of me?'

A shy person deep down, he considered the incident an invasion of his highly cherished privacy and from that time onwards he kept his own family in the dark about his activities with girlfriends unless he brought one home for approval. And that was rare enough for his parents to know that when he did it was someone he considered special. They knew he slipped out at nights, and after he bought a motorcycle they would occasionally see him flashing by with a girl riding pillion bound for Gullane Beach where he would join other friends to swim and play on the sands. But when he moved to London they knew little of his affairs as he struggled to make a living as an actor.

They know nothing, for example, of Shelley Winters who proved herself to be a friend in need when Sean could not find something like £150 to keep the roof of his mews flat over his head.

'I insisted on lending him the cash and Sean kept the repayment as my spending money any time I needed it in London,' she says. 'Years later when he was passing through New York we met up with Sammy Davis Jnr and his wife who was wearing the most marvellous fur coat in a champagne colour. I kept saying what a wonderful coat it was and the next night a similar coat was delivered to me with a note saying: "With interest on your money – Sean." It was a lovely gesture. And you know I'd never have thought he'd do a thing like that because he had this reputation for being tight with his money. Because he was Scottish, I suppose.'

Preferring male company in public he also had the reputation among girls with whom he kept company in private of being 'a man's man'. As one of his girlfriends of pre-Bond days puts it: 'Sean preferred standing at the bar drinking beer with his mates. When I arrived he would turn on the charm to establish his territorial rights and then leave me talking with friends while he went back to the bar. Some fifteen or twenty minutes before we were due to leave he would come back again to make sure that when I left it would be with him. Of course I always did. I was too fascinated by his great hairy chest and his beautiful biceps to remember what we talked about.'

Another visitor to the mews flat, an actress friend of Joe Kaufman's who was invited there for dinner, says: 'I think Sean, like so many men, puts women into two categories: those who do and those who don't. It was said that he didn't choose to spend his time with women unless it was going to be worth his while. Sexually, that is. But it so happens that I didn't want to go to bed with him that night and he wasn't a bit put out by it. He simply shrugged his shoulders, cooked a perfect meal for us both and we spent a great evening just talking and listening to music.'

The former model and film actress Sue Lloyd, now probably

better known for her continuing role as Mrs David Hunter in the television motel saga *Crossroads*, first met Sean in his hungry London years at the Buxton Club, a hide-out for actors just off Trafalgar Square that no longer exists. 'That first time he saw me home and stayed the night. We cuddled up in my bed and went to sleep. Just that. It was a matter of convenience with no desire involved.

'The second time was different. He and Diane Cilento were in the middle of one of their up-and-down periods. Sean came to a party without her and we got very merry. Once again he came back to my place and stayed the night and this time it was not just for convenience. All I can say is that he was warm, sweet and lovable. A big, cuddly, teddy bear of a man. Three months later he married Diane.'

Sean Connery had finally found the house he was seeking. A former convent, at one time occupied by nuns of the Order of Adoractrices, it was a four-storey building set in its own grounds, the only house in a cul-de-sac off Acton High Street. He bought it for £9,000 and was prepared to pay another £9,000 to convert it into a rambling, elegant home for himself and his bride-to-be.

He once called Diane Cilento 'the girl who has the most inner sex appeal for me' and having now decided on the house he told his parents that he would marry Diane when her divorce was final. The problem was that this would be in October, the same month that *Dr No* was due to be premiered in London with all the advance publicity and attendant ballyhoo confidently predicting a smash hit. They wanted a quiet wedding and a ceremony in London would probably be impossible but wherever it was he would let them know.

Meanwhile work went ahead on the house with Diane's artist sister Margaret going in most days to keep an eye on the builders. The chapel was being knocked into a 37-foot long L-shaped drawing room with six windows; there would be five bedrooms, a sunbathing balcony and a script learning room. And over the front door reached by a flight of nine steps would be the illuminated name sign: Acacia House. It did not sound like James Bond – not until one quiet Sunday afternoon when four little boys aged between nine and ten years old walked in and made their escape with a haul that included two cameras, an electric razor and some gramophone records. Sean had been camping out quietly in the unfinished house but was away when it happened. The newspapers reported: 'Four Boys Rob James Bond'. It was a pointer to what lay ahead. Already the character was overshadowing the actor.

Apart from this, everything else had gone according to plan. In the divorce courts Diane Cilento had been granted a decree on the grounds of her husband's desertion. At an earlier hearing the judge had exercised discretion in respect of her admitted adultery and she was now free to marry again. Indeed, their close-knit coterie of friends fully expected them to, now that the barriers had been removed.

In the same month *Dr No* opened to a brisk business at the box-office that was not only putting smiles on the faces of Harry Saltzman and Cubby Broccoli. The paperback publishers of the Fleming thriller began to watch boggle-eyed as the book sales mounted with the success of the film. In Britain alone they would put out 1 million copies. In the U.S.A. it would be 4 million.

On the quayside at Gibraltar Sean Connery waited with gathering impatience and concern. He had a secret assignment and he had the special licence for it. A week earlier on the telephone he had told his father the time, date and place and stressed the secrecy of his mission which had absolutely nothing to do with Fleming's James Bond but absolutely everything to do with Sean Connery being taken for James Bond in the public eye.

This day, 29 November 1962, he had chosen to be married to Diane Cilento at Gibraltar Register Office. Everything had been arranged in the best cloak-and-dagger tradition but he was still waiting for the bride.

In fact Diane Cilento was also waiting – across the water in Algeciras where a policeman had forgotten to stamp her passport. By the time it was in order she had missed the ferry.

'Sean must have thought I'd stood him up,' she sys. 'When I failed to arrive he crossed back on the ferry and we returned to Gibraltar together.'

There, with two taxi drivers who signed their names as Garcia and Gonzales, witnesses to the brief ceremony, they were legally married, he for the first time at thirty-two and she for the second at the age of twenty-five.

Their wedding night was spent at the Rock Hotel and the following afternoon they set out for Spain's Costa del Sol by car. They had rented a villa for their honeymoon from the Marques de las Torres, a villa entwined with leaves which provided a romantic setting in the warm sunshine.

Their nearest neighbour was Manolo Gonzalez, a bull-fighter who was the son-in-law of the Marques and had a villa opposite. Their closest companion was Giovanna, Diane's now five-year-old daughter known in the Connery family as 'Gigi'. For both of them work lay ahead. Sean was due to film in Turkey and Rome, and Diane had been commissioned to translate an Italian play for London's Royal Court Theatre, Pirandello's *The Rules of the Game*. As Sean said: 'You can't be married to a serious actress and a girl with serious appetites like Diane and have an eye for other women.'

He meant it. Meanwhile he fell in love with the Spanish weather and with Marbella in particular.

7

Diane Cilento

Like some well-oiled publicity machine the wheel of fortune now began to turn for Sean Connery. The year 1963 was barely nine days old when he walked into the casino at St Vincent in northern Italy and inside a few minutes won £10,000 at the roulette table. He was playing No. 17 and supposedly using a system devised by Ian Fleming for James Bond. However, there was also a photographer conveniently ready and waiting to take a shot of the gilt-edged Bond smiling above his stack of chips before he left with three glamorous starlets in tow.

With *Dr No* beginning to make its first million and the second Bond film *From Russia With Love* about to go into production, the image-makers were wasting no time and sparing no effort. The casino management was quoted. 'The biggest win of the season,' they said. Ian Fleming was consulted. 'I've used the method myself,' he said, 'but I'm dashed if I have picked up as much cash as that. Tell him I expect a fair split.' The newspapers were delighted.

Four days later the same starlets, Seyna Seyn, Olivia Hill and Gillian Evanne, were pictured arriving in Rome, reportedly for screen tests, accompanied by Sean Connery. The four of them were sitting in a restaurant when students kidnapped the girls, holding them for three hours and releasing them after a ransom of kisses all round. Everyone was delighted with this display of Bond-baiting with the exception of the police who had been called in and the newly-wed Mrs Sean Connery who had preoccupations of her own.

She, too, was in Rome, but keeping a low profile. At this moment in her life her desire for privacy was understandable. With their marriage less than two months old she had just presented Sean Connery with a son, a boy they called Jason, who was born in the Eternal City on 12 January 1963.

Perhaps she should have been grateful that the publicity spotlight was turned elsewhere at the time, concentrating on the gambling and womanizing James Bond image. However, although she understood the demands made on stars to promote a product, she had little use for publicity in general and practically no use at all for publicists in particular. 'If judging beauty competitions means being a star then I want no part of it,' she once said. Indeed, in order to appreciate Sean Connery's hardening attitudes towards the press over the coming years, the almost obsessive desire to protect his private life from the prying eye, it is also necessary to know something of the glamorous woman he had married.

Long before she married him, the slim and beautiful green-eyed Diane Cilento had been hailed as a star both in films and the theatre. And her attitudes towards stardom and certain people in the film business found a ready and responsive echo in this man who valued his privacy.

They had a great deal in common. Both had had no formal education beyond the age of fourteen. Both had known what it was like to be broke and lonely in London. As an out-of-work actress, Diane Cilento had once sold programmes at a circus in Olympia. She had also been what she called a G-woman, a fairground showman's decoy for drawing the crowds. She could have written home for help but felt she wanted to make her own way. When she joined a theatrical company after drama-school training in New York it was as an assistant electrician for one-night stands.

There was nothing phoney about her, a characteristic that came high on the list of Sean Connery's requirements in a human being. When someone described her as 'mercurial' she snapped: 'So is everybody who has a publicist.' When they called her 'unpredictable' she answered: 'Who is predictable, except for publicists?'

In fact she was unpredictable by temperament and unconventional by nature. She once said of herself: 'I'm a rebel. I hate conforming. I love to stir things up. I like having fun. They say I'm rude because I won't tolerate people I dislike. I would sooner be true to myself and say what I think.'

This is perhaps why a close friend of the couple at the time said: 'Don't let Diane's warm smile fool you. She can be just like the moon and the sun. Cold as ice or hot as Hades, depending on which one she elects to turn towards you.'

She had been in films since she was eighteen, but it was her stage performance in *The Big Knife* in 1954 that so impressed the late Sir Alexander Korda that he put her under an £11,000 film contract. She was just twenty. A year later she so impressed the New York critics as Helen of Troy in the Broadway production of *Tiger at the Gates* that director Elia Kazan offered her the leading role in *Baby Doll*, the film that made Carroll Baker famous. Committed to the play, she turned him down. Later, when the film came out, she said she thought Carroll Baker was excellent in the part but found the film itself distasteful. 'Some people enjoy watching a snake play with and then kill a rabbit. I don't. In *Baby Doll* the husband didn't stand a chance. I don't think that's fair. It's not my idea of a fair fight.'

She was an extrovert who rode a motor scooter around town, who smoked cigars, and in one eating place decided that the wine on the adjoining table was more exciting than her own. So she leaned across, borrowed the bottle, poured herself a glass and returned the wine to the startled customer with a nonchalant *Sal]uté*, spoken in her notably seductive voice. Her voice enchanted many with its fascinating huskiness, a quality she later discovered was due to nodes on her vocal chords.

She was just as impulsive when it came to her first marriage. 'I'd been telling publicists I was going to marry an Italian writer but they didn't take any notice,' she says. Perhaps it was because she did not tell them when.

It was two days after she married Andrea Volpe at Kensington Register Office in February 1955 that the news broke. She claimed they had known one another for three weeks when he proposed to her in Rome on the Via Gloria.

'I must have been mad,' she says in retrospect, 'but in those days it was the thing to do, to get married.'

Certainly the marriage seemed doomed almost from the start. They were hardly ever together for any length of time. When she opened in *Tiger at the Gates* on Broadway he was in London translating for Sir Alexander Korda. When she was in London, he appeared to be in Rome. In fact, no one quite knew what Andrea Volpe did for a living. He was twenty-three and variously described as a writer, an engineering student, a journalist, a trainee film director and, as though to rub salt in the wounds of a girl who had no time for stardom's trappings, a film publicist.

It was in March 1957 during the pre-London run of *Zuleika*, a musical based on Sir Max Beerbohm's *Zuleika Dobson* in which Diane was starring, that Andrea Volpe went to Room 242 in the Randolph Hotel in Oxford to discover his wife in a state of hysteria. Her wrists were slashed and there was a broken glass on the floor. It was one o'clock in the morning and she had not long returned from the theatre. He knew there had been problems with the show both in Manchester, where she had not allowed him to visit her, and in Wolverhampton, but he did not realise how close his wife had come to breaking point. He summoned a doctor and managed to keep the incident quiet for a few days while she recuperated in a nursing home.

She surfaced in Palermo, Sicily, where she told reporters who had tracked her down in a beach hotel that there was no question of a break-up between her husband and herself. 'The trouble was the show,' she said. 'There were so many changes I couldn't stand it any longer. I was told of some of the changes in the script only five minutes before I was due to go on stage for curtain-up and I thought it would ruin my career. I got to the point where I could stick knives in people without a qualm. Back in my hotel I threw a tantrum. I broke a glass and went into the bathroom. I stood there with the glass in my hand – and I don't remember any more. My husband came into the room but he was too late. He was furious with me. He called a doctor because my wrists were bleeding and the next day he got me into a nursing home.'

She was now simply taking things quietly and considering what to do with her future. A few days later she moved from Sicily to Rome. There she stayed with her husband and his family, who obviously felt there was an Italian answer to this problem of a career wife. When she returned to England to finish filming a picture called *The Truth About Women* some eight weeks later, she announced she was expecting a baby. And she planned to have it in Australia because she wanted her child to have a choice of Australian citizenship. She also wanted more time to think things out in the bosom of her own family who had always given her freedom of action. Her husband stayed in Rome awaiting his call-up for military service with the Italian army.

'My trouble now,' she confided, 'is that I have no ambition. I've reached the point where you see through showbusiness and think: "What does it matter?" The public? I do not care what the public think. I am not in love with the public.'

This, then, was the attitude of mind of the volatile Miss Diane Cilento when, two months later in August 1957, she met Sean Connery for the first time. They had been teamed together for a television production of *Anna Christie* and it was not, according to her, love at first sight.

'It was a whole year before we fell in love,' she says. 'He was virtually unknown and not nearly as attractive in those early days.'

The following month she flew out to Australia, leaving Sean Connery in possession of her motor scooter, and in December she gave birth to a daughter, Giovanna Margaret, in a Brisbane hospital. She returned to England in mid-February the next year and settled into a flat in Bayswater with her two-month-old baby. One of her first visitors was Sean Connery bearing a bunch of daffodils. She greeted him warmly and over the course of the next three or four years, bridging separations caused by the working pattern of their lives, the romance flourished. It was not very long before she realized that her marriage to Andrea Volpe was over, but it was a much longer wait before she decided to divorce him on the grounds of desertion.

The divorce was handled by Lord Goodman and the hearing was one of the longest undefended suits in the history of the divorce court. She spent twenty-five minutes in the witness box answering questions before the judge decided it was a case in which the final decree should be speeded up.

Such was the background to Diane Cilento's long-running affair with Sean Connery which led to their get-away-from-it-all marriage in Gibraltar and the birth of a son so soon after their honeymoon.

In February 1963 the Connery family moved into their new home in Acton, where they had installed a housekeeper and organized a nursery for Jason. Diane Cilento's daughter Giovanna had her own room, and in the comfortably furnished drawing room where twenty-five nuns had once knelt in prayer at chapel there was piped-in hi-fi equipment, a twenty-three-inch television set and a drinks cabinet. That part of the room which formed an L-shape accommodated a desk where the master of the house planned to cope with his accounts and correspondence.

It seemed to be the perfect setting for a stable home life away from the hassles of the film set, but in truth Connery had little time to spare for domesticity. He faced his second Bond film in his six-picture contract, but he also had plans of his own. He had no intention of being devoured by the Bond image. To avoid the dangers of type-casting he decided to set up his own film company. His first production, he thought, would be a comedy to be made in Australia the following September starring his wife and himself.

As a Scotsman Sean Connery knew very well that when you cast your bread (in this case a reported £100,000) upon the waters you first make sure the tide is coming in. And it was Terence Young, the director of *From Russia With Love* who shrewdly observed: 'Most actors are simple but complicated. Sean is uncomplicated but not simple.'

8

From Russia With Love

Terence Young had a problem most men would have regarded as a labour of love. Bond addicts, and they included John F. Kennedy, that charismatic President of the United States who had publicly nominated Ian Fleming's *From Russia With Love* among his ten favourite books, were raving over their first glimpse of the original 007 girl, Ursula Andress. Now Terence Young's task was to find a beauty with similar impact. He spent some days poring over photographs of 200 girls anxious to find a niche in the 007 harem, and finally his choice fell upon Daniela Bianchi, a Roman golden blonde.

She was to play Tania, the Russian cypher clerk and hatchet girl who ended up sharing a sleeping car with Bond on a transcontinental express, simply attired in a black velvet neck ribbon. In the event it was generally considered by connoisseurs that she was neither as erotic nor as athletically exciting as Ursula Andress, whose appearance in the first Bond film was to establish her as an international sex symbol.

Furthermore, the Bianchi voice, which sounded husky and sexy on screen, was not even her own. It had to be dubbed and was in fact the voice of Barbara Jefford, the Shakespearian actress who had appeared on Broadway with Diane Cilento in *Tiger at the Gates*.

To Sean Connery, who had been taking lessons to sharpen up his golf, this was just about par for the course. He had for some time been aware that he was in a phoney business where people were accepted for their bank balance and their success at the box-office, but not for themselves. From the outset he had been irreverent about Bond and his standards because he saw them both as a huge slice of hokum. He could not have treated the business in any other way since he himself had to conceal his naturally balding pate by wearing a 'rug', or toupee – in fact a series of carefully contrived hairpieces (which he detested) depending on whether he was in action as 007 making war or 007 making love.

As for the stunts that were creating the superman image – well, take the black widow spider that was introduced into his bed in *Dr No*. They had experimented with rubber toys at first and then they had used a real live tarantula whose bite could be lethal. For the shot they had placed a glass screen over his chest as protection, although they knew he could not bear anything furry that scuttled. He hated creepy-crawly creatures and he had felt damned uncomfortable throughout that sequence, which he had known to be a key one. Then they'd discovered that the glass reflected in the camera lens and the whole scene had to be re-shot using his stunt man.

'The whole thing was a joke,' he says. 'An entertainment. Anyone who took it seriously needed a headshrinker.'

However, Connery was shrewd and calculating enough to know that it was a joke which had all the signs of keeping Messrs Broccoli and Saltzman laughing all the way to the bank vaults. And he was determined not to be left too far behind. He realized that in James Bond there was the opportunity of a lifetime and in his book opportunity knocks only once. You have to grab it while it is there. It is what those who do not grab it call luck.

Cubby Broccoli would have agreed with those sentiments. The already affluent Cubby knew all about luck. His own good fortune had begun with a windfall. Or rather two windfalls. The first was when his grandmother died and left him $1 million. The second was when he met a character called Irving Allen, born Applebaum, in London, England. Allen, one-time scriptwriter for British International Pictures, had a property. Cubby had the money. All they needed was a star and they were in business. So they went into partnership and wined and dined Alan Ladd, small in stature but then big at the box-office, and his wife Sue Carroll who was at that time one of Hollywood's most prestigious agents.

Over the cigars Irving Allen asked: 'What'll you take for Alan's contract, Sue?'

Without batting a false eyelash she replied: 'A million dollars.'

Irving coolly flicked the ash from his cigar.

'Write her a cheque, Cubby,' he said.

For sheer style it would have been difficult to match and Cubby Broccoli's nerve was equal to the occasion. A high-rolling gambler by nature, he had, without turning one hair of his now elegantly greying head, signed away all the real money they had. That had been the beginning of Warwick Films, which was launched with *The Red Beret*, starring Alan Ladd.

The partnership between the affable Cubby and the rather more abrasive Harry Saltzman began in much the same way. Saltzman held the expiring option on the Bond books and Broccoli could rustle up the finance necessary to put them on the screen.

For a man catapulted into international fame, Sean Connery appeared to take things remarkably calmly at this stage. He was something of a strategist, learning to take a long, cool view of what lay ahead and plan accordingly.

'If I'd been twenty-five and unknown, Bond might have ruined me,' he reasoned. 'I might have got myself eternally typed or jumped at any offer that came along. I turned a number of them down, especially television series, which included the lead in *Maverick*. They might have earned me a fortune but they would have finished me as an actor. It was as an actor that I wanted to survive. I knew that handled the right way Bond would make me rich, give me security and still leave me free to make other films and pick my own parts.'

In this he had the support of his wife, Diane Cilento, who felt that the James Bond role was less than he was capable of as an actor but who could also see that for some appreciable time she would have to play second fiddle to a husband who was rapidly becoming identified with a cult figure. She was not particularly concerned about the girls in the life of James Bond because they were not entering the life of Sean Connery and she felt reasonably secure in her own intelligence and physical attraction. As Stanley Sopel says: 'It was obvious to everyone that Sean adored her. He thought she was the greatest thing since – well, since sliced bread.'

He used the cliché as the finest accolade anyone could bestow. 'Not even Ursula Andress, who got along with Sean well enough, stood a chance by comparison with Cilento. She was and still is a very lovely lady.'

Without any conceit Diane Cilento said of herself at this time: 'Men have always been interested in me. I've always taken it for granted. But it's dangerous to be obsessed with your own good looks. Beauty-conscious women seem to miss so much in life. They are forever worrying if a nail breaks or wasting their best years under a hair drier. Sean likes me to be natural. After all he knows me. He doesn't want me to be an ornament and neither do I. He has a good taste in clothes and that means a plain taste. Elegant but not flashy. And I understand him thoroughly. I buy all his ties for him, play golf with him and do most of the things that he does. I can even do judo with him.'

This togetherness extended to being on location with him in Turkey for *From Russia With Love*, where there were innumerable problems. The weather turned sour on them and they could not get the right type of boats for the beach scenes. Connery flew back from Istanbul for a ninety-minute mission at London's White City where he played inside left for a showbusiness eleven against the Internationals Club, a testimonial match for Alec Farmer who had spent thirty years as a player and trainer at Queen's Park Rangers. It took him back to his *South Pacific* touring days when he had been offered terms with Manchester United. He loved the game still but he was now hooked on golf, which was to become one of the ruling passions of his life. As he said: 'You need twenty-one other fellows for a game of football, but it's easy to get a game of golf.'

Glen Mason, the singer and a friend, had told him about an exclusive golf clinic for Top People which was set in a squash court in the heart of London's Belgravia, and Connery's dentist Ian Caldwell, who also happened to be the English champion, arranged for him to take lessons there. Connery had valid reasons. One was that he would be faced in the not-too-distant future with a key scene in *Goldfinger*: the famous Goldfinger-Bond golf duel at 'Royal St Mark's'. Although he could play the game after a fashion (he had been a member of the Stage Golfing Society), he needed specialist coaching to appear convincing. He was not even a handicap player. However, there was a more powerful and compelling reason, one that concerned his temperament and personal make-up. He relished competitiveness and did not enjoy anything unless he did it well.

In time, with a reconstructed swing, he brought the same streak of ruthlessness to the game as did actor Robert Shaw, who played his blond adversary in *From Russia With Love*. Neither man could bear to be beaten.

'Golf,' says Connery, 'is the greatest test of temperament I know. No game upsets me or elates me as much as golf. And sixty per cent of what golf is all about is who you play with. Frankly, I don't like playing with women.'

Back in Istanbul Terence Young and his crew managed to wrap up most of the production, which was well over schedule at this stage, just two days before a revolution broke out. It had been a project dogged by setbacks all the way. The film had already gone £200,000 over its budget of $1.9 million, and scenes that could no longer be shot in Turkey were finished on location in Scotland, on the Firth of Lorne in Argyllshire. There the problems continued. Terence Young and his assistant Michael White crashed into the sea in a helicopter and suffered minor injuries, and Daniela Bianchi was involved in a car crash which left her with a badly bruised face. As for Sean Connery, the brief return to his homeland resulted in a bout of flu, but with seventy-two technicians waiting around he was forced to carry on.

'Have you ever tried accommodating seventy-three people in a tiny Scottish village?' he said tetchily to a reporter incautious enough to ask him how he felt on returning to his native heath.

He had wanted the film to finish on schedule because he was committed to making a picture with Gina Lollobrigida, called *Woman of Straw*, and had planned to spend some time with his wife and family between the two. Now the two productions were threatening to kaleidoscope and his only compensation was that he was on a special rate because *From Russia With Love* had run into overtime.

Money meant a great deal to Sean Connery, who was on a salary and felt he was entitled to every single penny he could get. 'Talent isn't fed on an empty stomach,' he growled. He also felt that his contribution to the Bond films was at least as great as that of his employers.

From an actor's point of view the character of James Bond had presented formidable problems. As Connery puts it: 'He has no mother. He has no father. He doesn't come from anywhere and he hadn't been anywhere before he became 007. He was born – kerplump – thirty-three years old. So I had to breathe life into an idol. I saw him as a complete sensualist, his senses highly tuned and awake to everything. He liked his wine, his food, his women. He's quite amoral. I particularly liked him because he thrived on conflict. But more than that I think I gave him a sense of humour.'

Connery often contributed throw-away lines to the script. This was certainly apparent in *From Russia With Love*, which opened in London in 1963. There was Lotte Lenya sliding on a vicious knuckleduster and belting an unflinching Robert Shaw in the stomach and saying: 'He seems fit enough.' And there was Lotte Lenya being shot by Daniela Bianchi when trying to kick Bond with a poisoned dagger concealed in her boot and Bond saying, 'To coin a phrase – she's had her kicks.' Even the bedroom scene with Bianchi was memorable. Finding the bare-shouldered beauty in his bed, Bond solemnly shakes her hand – 'Dr Livingstone, I presume?'

Lines that look almost banal in print took on another dimension in the film, which almost immediately began to break all box-office records. There were queues everywhere when it opened in the United States. The impact was enormous and the coffers of Messrs Saltzman and Broccoli began to run with what looked like molten gold.

It was at this point that Sean Connery felt that if he was to continue playing Bond something would have to be done about his share. He wanted a piece of the action. More, he wanted recognition that he was just as much a partner in this money-spinning enterprise as they were.

Terence Young says: 'Sean wanted to be a full partner with Cubby and Harry. He wanted it because he felt it was his due. There they were, Cubby and Harry, sitting on $50 million or so and Sean outside the door calculating that maybe a third of it should be his.'

And Cubby Broccoli admits: 'It was after those first two films that our relationship deteriorated. He got mad at us about expenses early on and he became sick and tired of us later.'

9

The Image Takes Root

There is one line in every Bond picture that remains the same. Implicit in it is the suggestion of menace and mayhem and murder to come: *My name is Bond. James Bond.* The words are calculated to send a frisson of excitement and expectancy through the ranks of paying customers at the box office but they have an altogether different effect on Roger Moore, the actor who became the latter-day Bond. He admits: 'I hate having to say that line because every time I say it I think of Sean.'

It is understandable because no one could hope to invest those six simple words with quite the same quality as Sean Connery, suggesting that beneath the suave approach lies the cold, innate cruelty of a man with a licence to kill. It is why Connery himself says: 'I am not ashamed of the Bond films. Quality is not only to be found at the Old Vic, and portraying Bond is just as serious as playing Macbeth.' As he had already played Macbeth in a Canadian production before going to work on *Dr No* he knew what he was talking about.

Terence Young understood Connery's attitude. 'He was an extraordinarily good actor before he came to us for the first time and he also knew his classics.' So it was his contribution as an actor that Sean Connery was determined would not go unrewarded. Furthermore, he was adamant that he would not be devoured by the Bond image or have it used as a peg on which others could hang out their own publicity.

I remember him standing by an ornamental lake in the grounds of Pinewood studios savouring his by now customary cigar when a curvy blonde flounced by bouncing her jaunty buttocks. He did not even look up, just kept smoothly drawing on his cigar.

Obviously disgruntled by this total failure to recognize her sexy presence the blonde returned, accompanied by wolf-whistles from appreciative technicians and shadowed by a photographer, camera poised for the moment of confrontation. As she walked by the second time she said brightly: 'D'you want me to take my clothes off again?'

Without glancing at her or removing the cigar from between his lips he murmured: 'Of course.' There was no movement and another frustrated photographer bit the dust.

In October 1963, when he was involved with Gina Lollobrigida and Sir Ralph Richardson in filming *Woman of Straw*, he acquired what many regarded as the latest in status symbols at that time. He was nominated for the post of Rector of Edinburgh University. To some people this was rather better value than a mention in the Birthday Honours List or an invitation to a royal garden party. It was the IN thing to be. There might even be an honorary doctorate of laws at the end of it. His opponents were fellow actors Peter Ustinov and James Robertson Justice, Dr Julius Nyerere, then President of Tanganyika, and Yehudi Menuhin.

However, he was left in no doubt that it was James Bond they thought they were voting for and not Sean Connery, although he had been born in that city. A banner draped across a statue of Sir Walter Scott read: 'Great Scott, it's Ustinov.' Flights of balloons boasting 'Justice is Best' floated over the city, but it was a plain '007' that was splashed on walls and footpaths. 'Who's Sean Connery?' asked one student. 'I'm for James Bond.'

He told newspapermen: 'I am Sean Connery, a serious actor with interests besides Bond, and if you keep calling me Bond or 007 then my chances of becoming rector won't be so good. The lads nominated me and I was only too willing to accept. It's an honour you know.'

It was an honour that remained unfulfilled. Connery was philosophical. When asked about the future and what it held for him at this stage he said thoughtfully: 'I suppose more than anything else I'd like to be an old man with a good face. Like Hitchcock. Or Picasso. They've worked hard all their lives, but there's nothing weary about them. They never wasted a day with the sort of nonsense that clutters up a life. They know that life is not just a bloody popularity contest. For now I'm reasonably content with what I'm doing. After all, I can kill any s.o.b. in the world and get away with it; I've got the powers of the greatest governments in the world behind me; I eat and drink nothing but the very best; and I also get the loveliest ladies in the world. What could be better?'

He knew very well what could be better. His pre-Bond period had been crucial to him. Having been thrown into a series of second-rate Hollywood films, an experience he likened to 'a man walking through a swamp in a bad dream', he had done just about everything the business had to offer: hoofing, movies, Shakespeare, television, the legitimate theatre. And it had given him what he needed most: mastery of his craft. True, it had made him somewhat bitter, but then he had every intention of having the last laugh.

To say that he had been entirely happy making *Woman of Straw* as a get-away-from-Bond picture would have been a lie. He could be abrasive about other people's temperament and insiders suggest that he shudders still at the memory of playing opposite the voluptuous Lollo. There had been an occasion during the filming when he was required to slap her face and unintentionally gave her a cut and swollen mouth. The director sent her home and later he telephoned to apologize. 'You only have to be an inch out in your calculations,' he explained, 'and I was. It was a fair old belt she got and she felt the blow, but she took it very well.'

He hoped for rather better things when he kept a date with Hitchcock in November 1963 to team in a new spine-chiller *Marnie*, with Tippi Hedren taking over the role that Princess Grace of Monaco had been offered and turned down. 'Hitch called me and asked me to be in his film,' Connery says. 'I told him to send a script and that I'd let him know if I accepted his offer. He said it was nonsense my asking to see a script; that Cary Grant had never asked to see a script. I told him I wasn't Cary Grant and that I never took a role unless I knew what I had to do and say. I got the part.'

This kind of high-handedness, which was said to have shocked Hollywood where Hitchcock was revered, gave rise to stories about Sean Connery's big-headedness and unco-operative attitudes. Such criticism he shrugged off on broad shoulders. In fact, the technicians on *Marnie* were so impressed with Connery's sheer professionalism on set as an actor who understood their problems that they made a collection at the end of the film and bought him a $1,000 watch as a token of their appreciation.

He took pride in the almost unprecedented gesture because he felt he had been accepted as a fellow craftsman. As he says: 'There are 100 people involved in putting you up there on screen. The trouble with some stars is that they develop heads as big as their close-ups. I've never really believed it's me up there on the wide screen. Just a guy with the same features and talking slightly posh.' His private voice has always had a more pronounced Scottish burr and he talked and joked with the technicians in language they readily understood, but it was his thoughtfulness that left its indelible mark.

In this he may well have been influenced by his wife Diane Cilento who had a similar relationship with studio crews. During her early Pinewood days she would rarely be found sharing a table in the elegantly panelled dining room with other stars, preferring instead to spend the lunch hour hobnobbing with the electricians and carpenters in the canteen.

While Connery was making the Hitchcock picture she flew to Hollywood to be with him, taking with her their son Jason, now little more than twelve months old. They were at a reception together when their English nanny reported that the boy was unwell. They left hurriedly and discovered he had swallowed water while learning to swim. Asked whether he did not think that a boy scarcely a year old was too young to take to the water, his father said: 'I don't think so. They start them at three months old over here.' He was unperturbed, remembering his own upbringing and the way his father had taught him to swim.

Sean Connery was still working on *Marnie* in February 1964 when he received a special award from the Variety Club of Great Britain for 'creating the screen role of James Bond', and in the same month he was holding out for new terms to be agreed before he would commit himself to do the new Bond film *Goldfinger*. Cubby Broccoli, who had already announced him as the star of the latest Bond film, due to start production the following month, flew to Hollywood to discuss details with him. No one was saying what they were but Connery said it concerned his artistic control of the picture.

'If we can't come to terms,' Connery went on, 'I don't know whether I'll do the film, although we'll have to cross that bridge when we come to it.'

At this stage in their deadlocked negotiations the fate not only of *Goldfinger* but of future Bond films was in the balance. Connery wanted to discuss contracts for these and Messrs Broccoli and Saltzman had just had something of a shock to the nervous system.

Indeed, what looked very much like a piranha fish had been dropped into their goldfish bowl of gilt-edged guppies.

Some weeks previously, in December 1963, Kevin McClory, an extrovert Irishman who had been born as excess baggage in a farm cart but had since developed a taste for the high life, having wooed and wed the heiress Bobo Sigrist, had won a High Court action against author Ian Fleming, financier John Bryce and the publishers Jonathan Cape Ltd. He received £35,000 damages and £17,500 costs in settlement of his claim and was granted the sole screen and dramatic rights of the novel *Thunderball*.

In court McClory and writer Jack Whittingham claimed they were the original authors of the book, on which they had worked with Fleming. In court also, with a watching brief as the interested third party, was the Broccoli-Saltzman company Eon Productions. Stanley Sopel says: 'Fleming pulled out and then we made a deal in the corridors of the court whereby Fleming retained the literary rights and McClory got the screen rights. Then Eon had to do a deal with McClory which meant that he would be the producer of the next Bond film to be made after *Goldfinger*, which would be *Thunderball*.'

Since the High Court action McClory had begun to travel the world in search of a challenger to Connery for the role of Bond in his production and was dropping prestige names in his wake such as Laurence Harvey, Richard Burton, Peter O'Toole and Rod Taylor, to name but a few. This did not seem to bother Connery. He said nothing more in public about the progress of his *Goldfinger* negotiations but continued to fight for money in private.

According to Tom Carlisle, the American publicist on the film, the problems of what Sean Connery was to be paid for *Goldfinger* were resolved in an odd way. One day on the set Harold Sakata, a professional wrestler who had been brought in to play Oddjob, probably the best remembered of all Bond villains with his bowler hat, black jacket and striped trousers and a dead-pan expression, was required to give Connery a judo chop on the neck.

Sakata, an expert in his own field, who had been working with stunt man Bob Simmons, knew how to prevent a blow having the same devastating effect physically as it had visually, but in the event Connery slumped down in a heap, complained of a headache and left the set. 'I don't know what happened in his absence,' says Carlisle. 'All I know is that when he returned to work his contract had been completely re-negotiated. From then on Sean had a salary increase to £50,000, a piece of his own action and a percentage of the films, plus other fringe benefits.'

Goldfinger was a turning point for Connery. He appeared to have everything going for him. Professionally he had the money and the power and the prestige to negotiate his own terms with other producers. However, his home life, which he tried desperately and in most cases successfully to guard from the public gaze, was something else again. Connery was typical of his generation. By virtue of temperament and upbringing he was the provider, the man who went out and won the bread for his wife and children back home and needed freedom to action while he was doing it. He was an individual who, to all intents and purposes was self-sufficient; who could cook his own meals if necessary and who needed space in which to operate. 'I cannot be with someone all the time,' he says, 'not even in the same house. It is too restricting. There are times when I have to be alone to be myself, study scripts, whatever.'

In Diane Cilento he had a wife whom he loved as a woman and whom he respected as an actress but she had a mind of her own and a career she was determined to pursue despite the Bond image which overshadowed them both. She could not settle into cosy retreat as a wife and mother, a docile handmaiden at the master's beck and call when needed. That would be another kind of bondage. And while the name James Bond was on everyone's lips she had gone out and won an Academy Award nomination for her portrayal of the slut in the film *Tom Jones*.

Life in the Connery household was not going to be easy for either of them from now on.

10

Fighting the Image

The American journalist Pete Hamill was in a London pub listening to the press agent who, having taken a furtive survey of the handful of drinkers present, stabbed what Hamill describes as the beer-and-onion scented air with his cigarillo. 'Sean Connery?' he said in a strangled voice. 'You want my honest opinion of Sean Connery?' He finished his whisky and soda with a gulp before beginning to talk in what started out as sober, measured tones but ended almost like a puppy's cry for help. 'Sean Connery is a great, big, conceited, untalented, wooden-headed *ninny*!' With that he banged his empty glass down violently on the bar and flipped his cigarillo over one shoulder. 'That's what *I* think of Mister Sean Connery.'

It says something for Mr Hamill's objectivity that he did not take these heartfelt words at face value but hot-footed it down to Pinewood studios the following day where in a draughty corner on Stage D he talked to a group of technicians preparing another scene for *Goldfinger*. A camera operator who had worked on all three Bond films peered through a view-finder before turning slowly and squinting into the overhead lights. 'Sean Connery,' he told Hamill, who was anxious to get another side of the story, 'is one of the classiest actors I've ever worked with. This guy is a real man. In this business you don't come across many of *them*.'

It was a measure of Connery's status as a film actor that he could refuse to discuss his home life or to admit photographers across the threshold of his home and get away with it. Terence Young told Hamill: 'Sean could be the biggest star in movies since Gable, but he doesn't give a damn for the ancillary assets of being a star. It's not that he's ungrateful. It's just that he's too concerned with personal integrity. A hell of a lot of people don't like Sean because of this.'

It was this maverick streak in Connery which appealed to his fellow actors but infuriated the publicity men who were increasingly thwarted as interest in their star mounted with the popularity of the films. *Dr No* was well on its way to making £2 million at the box office and *From Russia With Love* was rapidly making more, having taken first place in the nation's affections according to a survey of 2,300 British cinemas by New York's *Motion Picture Herald*. '*We* made him,' wailed one press agent, 'and now he treats us like *swine*.'

Connery had his reasons. 'My private life, or most of it, is my own business and I intend to keep it that way.' This was hardly surprising in view of the fact that even sophisticated journalists, when he did agree to see them, were asking ridiculous questions such as: 'What would you do on the other side of the Iron Curtain, Mr Bond?' Even worse, they had begun to plague his wife, asking her what it was like being married to a sexual athlete like James Bond.

There are times, indeed, when Diane Cilento was beginning to feel like two people and getting her identities mixed up from time to time. 'People ring up and say: "Is that Mrs James Bond?" and while the idea of being someone I'm not appals me I usually say "Yes" in the end because it's not worth arguing. Perhaps the easiest way to illustrate the difference between my two identities is to tell you what happens when I ring my bank manager. If I ring as Miss Cilento with a single account and then again as Mrs Sean Connery with a joint account you can measure the change in attitude because it is in thousands of pounds. Even though I was quite well known and could manage quite well before I married Sean. But it is because of Sean that I am now not just Mrs Sean Connery but Mrs James Bond at the same time. It's not only confusing. It can be humiliating.'

Connery himself, who had little time for the bright lights, the parties and other by-products of the film business, protested that too much had been made of his failure to conform to these well-established patterns. 'I just don't have time for all that jazz,' he explained. 'I've been working continuously for a year and a half and I don't see why I can't grab my relaxation where and when I can. I don't want my free time taken up with interviews. My job is to entertain, not seek the limelight for foolish antics and I hate being promoted as a product by the publicity machine.'

As one of his close friends put it: 'When Sean goes out it's to enjoy himself as Sean Connery the individual and to hell with the public and the studio.'

However, there were also those who said that when Sean Connery went out to enjoy himself he had barbed wire in his pockets because he was not exactly the fastest right hand in the business when it came to shelling out for a drink or a meal. Stanley Sopel was not among them. 'The man has bought me more lunches than I care to think about,' he says. 'He'd take me to one of the clubs in St James's when in London. The Eccentric was a favourite. And there were two reasons why he went to a club. In the first place it's a retreat where you cannot be buttonholed by the public as you can in a restaurant, and secondly, while the food is adequately good enough it is not nearly so expensive as in a restaurant.

'We had perfectly reasonable lunches and I never ever saw him sign a bill or give a credit card. Sean is a man who pays his way as he goes. I think the truth of the matter is simple enough. When he became conscious of the fact that he was on his way to becoming a very wealthy man he was determined to stay one. And to hell with freeloaders and what people thought. He did not have to flash his money about to impress or to prove anything to anyone, least of all himself. He is the least vain man I know.'

Denis Selinger, the agent, agrees. 'Sean doesn't throw his money around. He's careful with money and has become even more careful as time has gone by. I remember being in Lapland right on the Arctic Circle when the phone rang. It was about 5·30 in the morning. "Denis?" a voice said, "This is Sean." I was a bit bewildered at that hour. "Sean who?" I said. "Sean Connery."

'He proceeded to tell me about something that he felt was unfair, something that someone had done to him, and he went on and on to what was becoming a very lengthy, very one-sided and very expensive conversation. Suddenly there was a pause. "What is it Sean?" I said. "Denis," he said – he sounded quite shocked – "Denis, I've just realized I'm paying for this call." And he put the phone down. Click. Just like that.'

Sean Connery also had a very good memory for faces, particularly when it came to people who claimed his friendship in public places to enhance their own image. And he had no hesitation in putting them down if they were foolish enough to try it. There was a producer who shall be nameless who went up to him during the Bond period, greeting him in full view of a number of people and hugging him like the proverbial long-lost brother. Connery looked at him and removed the man's encircling friendly arm as though it was a poisonous snake. When he had uncoiled its alien length he said: 'Yes. I know you.' He spoke coolly and with distaste. 'You turned me down for a small part in 1958. And you didn't even give me a cup of tea.'

Ian Fleming was a sick man. In 1961 he had had a coronary thrombosis. He had been told to pace himself more carefully, cut down on his smoking and cut out altogether his favourite dish of scrambled eggs which went with his crispy bacon. Throughout the shooting of *Goldfinger*, however, he had continued to drink neat brandy as though it was iced water and bourbon mixed, and he drank it to the very last.

It was not long after the famous golf duel between James Bond and Auric Goldfinger, played out at Stoke Poges in Buckinghamshire, in which Bond, with £5,000 at stake, cheats his adversary and Oddjob crushes the offending ball in a symbolic gesture that Fleming suffered another heart attack which was to prove fatal. He remained conscious for three hours after the first searing pain and this gentlemanly chronicler of the ungentlemanly James Bond was urbane and courteous to the end. To the ambulancemen who sped him to the hospital he said: 'Thank you for all your help. I'm sorry to have been so much trouble to you chaps.'

It was August 1964 when he died, at the age of fifty-six.

There would be no more Bond stories from his pen but there was plenty of material to film and he had lived long enough to see the economic rewards of his books even if he had not been fit enough to have any real fun with his money. Boosted by the success of the films, the book sales had reached staggering numbers worldwide. Someone had stopped counting when they were selling more than sixty million copies in eleven languages, and Fleming felt he owed a debt of gratitude to Sean Connery, who had brought his fictional hero to life.

Goldfinger was a high-water mark in the Bond saga. United Artists had financed it with a budget of $2.9 million and it had been directed by Guy Hamilton, that debonair director whose idea, among others, it had been to have Oddjob's bowler hat equipped with a steel brim that could cut through any object with frightening ease. Curiously, the distributors of the film had not been convinced it would be a success. They grossly underestimated the gathering momentum of the Bond cult. In fact the film recouped its production costs in the United Kingdom alone and immediately started making money overseas like a private mint. In six months it took $45 million at the box office which, dollar for dollar, was a better return than *Star Wars*.

In September 1964, when *Goldfinger* was world premiered in London, a crowd of more than 5,000 surged in an excited, straining mass, craning their necks to see James Bond in the flesh of Sean Connery, but he was not there. He never attended any of his Bond premieres in this country. He spent that night quietly at home while it took 100 policemen to hold the crowd in check as they witnessed the arrival of Bond's girls: Honor Blackman, the *Avengers* girl turned Pussy Galore; Shirley Eaton, victim of a gold-spray job which gave her one of the more exotic exits from a Bond story; and Nadja Regin. They were mobbed, and such was the pressure that one special constable was heaved straight through a plate-glass window.

It is hardly surprising that Sean Connery was becoming rapidly disenchanted. Although he was gaining in prestige with every Bond film, his greatest desire was to escape becoming indelibly identified with the character. Which is why, in October 1964, as cinemagoers queued to see him in *Goldfinger*, he was a million miles away from the martini-shaken-with-mayhem world of James Bond. In Almeria, Spain, his hair close-cropped and wearing a moustache, all sophistication stripped away from his powerful frame, he played a tough, rebellious, busted R.S.M. being punished for striking an officer. This film, directed by Sidney Lumet who had made *Twelve Angry Men* and *Long Day's Journey Into Night*, was called *The Hill*.

Nothing he could have chosen could have been further away from the Bond character than this. It was a tough assignment. Wearing full army kit he and others in the cast had to run up a man-made hill thirty-five feet high built of concrete, rocks and sand. And Lumet asked his actors in the interests of authenticity to run up and down that hill at least six times if they could. It was a cruel test of stamina, especially for the portly Roy Kinnear who collapsed, and Connery himself, who pulled a tendon. Lumet said the story was based on

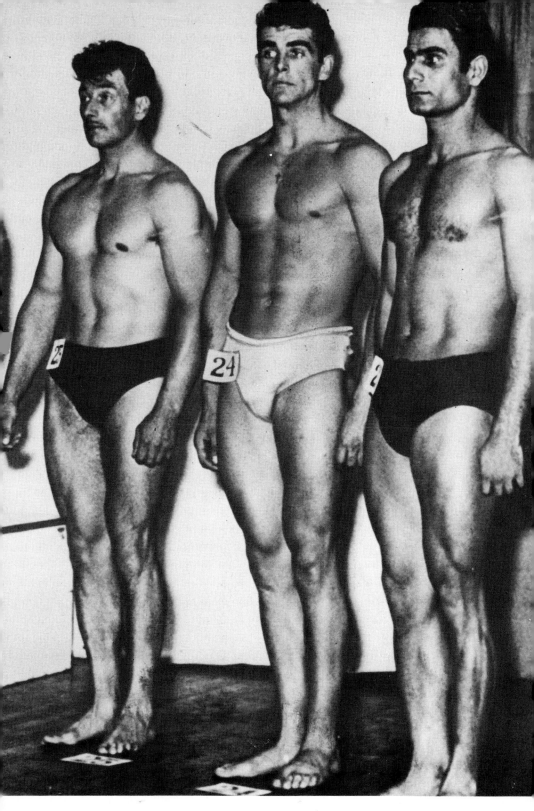

Connery (centre) as 'Mr Scotland' bidding to be 'Mr Universe'

Fountainbridge, Edinburgh. The tenement in which Connery used to live has now been pulled down

Darroch Secondary School. 'He was no great scholar. English was the only subject he appeared to be good at'

With Lana Turner in *Another Time, Another Place*, 1958

On honeymoon with Diane Cilento, 'the girl who has the most inner sex appeal for me', December 1962

Being fitted for a suit for *From Russia With Love*, March 1963

With Gert Frobe in *Goldfinger*, 1964

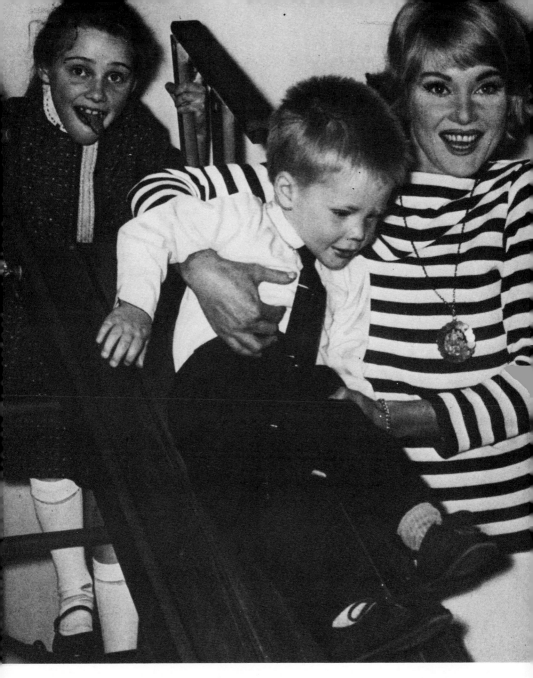

Diane Cilento and two-year-old Jason. Looking on is Giovanna, aged seven,
April 1965

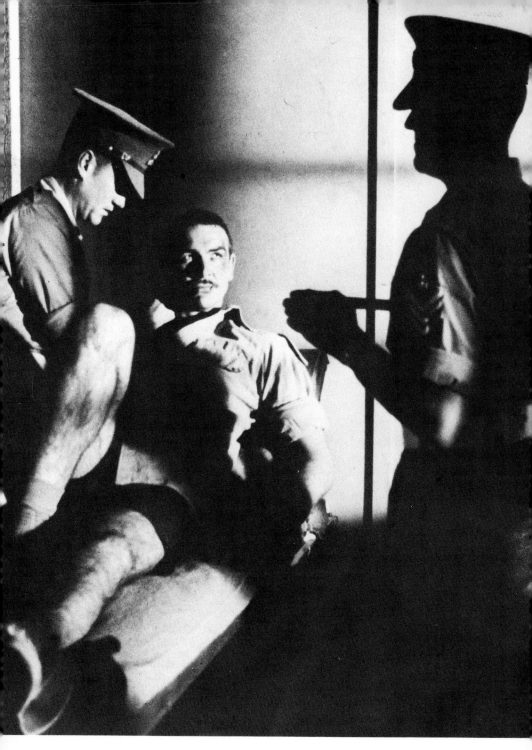

A scene from *The Hill*, 1965

fact. Running up and down a hill in full pack under a blazing sun was one of the many punishments devised for British soldiers by their fellow countrymen during the North African campaign. And Lumet was delighted with Connery's performance. 'Anyone who still thinks he can't act is in for one hell of a surprise,' he said.

It was while he was working in Spain that Kevin McClory announced that his world search for someone else to play Bond was at an end. 'There is no rival to Sean Connery as Bond,' he said. 'He is the only star who can project the Bond image.'

Connery was irritated. 'I'm not conscious of an image,' he insisted when told of McClory's decision and the reason for it. 'I play a part because I want to play it. Even if *The Hill* isn't a success – does it matter? Some of the finest films made haven't been commercial successes. You don't have to justify it. Frankly, I'd welcome someone else playing Bond. I know Richard Burton considered taking it on for *Thunderball* but I think it would be a crazy move for him. Bond is so completely successful that whatever anyone does now, they can't make him more so.'

He also knew that although he had temporarily exchanged 007 Agent James Bond for 421 Trooper Joe Roberts, he would be back to the pyjamas, the silken bedsheets and the well-cut suits before long. Meanwhile, he thought it would be a good idea to have a family Christmas at home.

He invited his mother and father, and his brother Neil and his wife to stay at Acton for the holiday, a quiet and festive reunion, and he had presents for them all. For his mother he had chosen a magnificent set of earrings with a matching necklace and brooch. It reminded them all of the time he had first bought her a brooch back in his boyhood days when he had spent half-a-crown of his hard-earned money – a fortune to him then – on the small token inscribed 'Mother'.

Throughout his later years, wherever he travelled, he did not forget his family, especially his parents. On his mother's birthday, for example, there would be a telegram, always with the same message: *Congratulations Mother on your 21st birthday – Love Tommy*. This year he had also sent her a present of £100 to mark the occasion. For his father that Christmas there was a cigarette lighter wrapped in two £10 notes. And for his brother's children there were two lace-trimmed romper suits he had brought back from Spain.

According to Neil Connery, his elder brother thoroughly enjoyed playing the host and family man, sliding young Jason on his bottom the length of the thirty-seven-foot living room where he skimmed along like a curling stone on ice.

It was a happy, carefree holiday before the onset of what was to be a remarkable New Year.

11
Bondmania

Only the very closest friends of Mr and Mrs Sean Connery sensed that all was not well with their marriage. And only to such treasured intimates who formed a tight circle of loyalty did they confide some of their difficulties. So it came as no great shock or surprise to the favoured few when Sean Connery moved out of the family home at Acton in March 1965, leaving Diane Cilento to look after the children, Giovanna, then aged seven, and Jason, who was two years old.

On the surface and to outsiders they still made the ideal couple. They had been seen in public together gracing the premiere of *The Yellow Rolls-Royce* in London only a few days after their family Christmas at home and again at the Royal Film show in February when the Queen Mother had personally singled out Sean Connery to tell him she thought his *Goldfinger* 'the best film she had ever seen'. At a party after the show they had danced together until the wee small hours.

The following day he was in Paris carrying out his promotional duties as Bond by attending the French premiere of *Goldfinger*. For this he was accompanied by a Mlle Claudine Auger, a former Miss France and before that an *au pair* in Mill Hill. She was destined to be the latest girl in his professional life as James Bond in *Thunderball*, in which she would make her entry bikini-clad on the back of a turtle.

At twenty-three she was an ambitious girl, married to a man of forty-seven, and she told those who were prepared to listen: 'In a Bond film you get noticed very fast. I know what I want and I think I could be foolish enough to give up my husband for a career.' This may or may not have been a philosophy she learned in Mill Hill, but Mlle Auger was not in the least worried about being caught with her quotes down. What she wanted was to be a star, as all the Bond girls did, and she had her first taste of star treatment when she and Sean Connery were confronted by a mob of 2,000 fans as they arrived for the French premiere of *Goldfinger*. Pushing aside a police guard, the crowd pulled both of them from their car, tearing the buttons from Connery's coat in the process. Two powerful bodyguards shouldered through the throng, forcibly lifted up the couple and pushed their way into the cinema. Minutes later everyone was smiling for the photographers. Another successful mission had been accomplished. This was the pattern of it with more to come.

Sean Connery and Diane Cilento had been living apart for about ten days when the news that they had decided on a trial separation in the hope of resolving their problems was made public. Richard Hatton, then Connery's agent, had denied reports that they were to separate. On the contrary, he had announced that they would make a film together. It was to be called *Big Country, Big Man* and it would be filmed later in the year in Diane Cilento's native Australia. It was now mid-March.

When reports of the couple's separation reached that film's producer, Doc Merman, in Sydney he gave the impression of a man about to climb up the nearest wall with frustration as he saw the project going up in smoke. 'If Connery and his wife are having personal problems it would be no use them trying to make a film together,' he said when he had recovered from the shock. 'They would only sour things up and make it impossible for the producer. I want a happy team. Can you imagine two married people who don't get along playing a love scene?'

Connery, who was then shooting love scenes at Pinewood with the Italian actress Luciana Paluzzi for *Thunderball*, refused to discuss the situation and Diane Cilento had nothing to say on the subject at that time. However, Connery much later made known his views on husband and wife teams. 'Diane and I are often asked why we don't make a film together. Frankly, it would be a bloody disaster. I don't go along with husband and wife double acts. I want a wife to go to bed with, not a script conference.'

The following month, on 13 April 1965, Diane Cilento flew to Nassau in the Bahamas where her husband was already at work. With her to the location she took the two children and a nanny. Sean Connery met them at the airport where he tucked young Jason under one arm and held his wife with the other. Refusing to discuss their previous estrangement they went straight to a bungalow set aside for them on what was called Love Beach and known locally as the Garden of Eden.

The first and obvious thought in everyone's mind was: have they kissed and made up, or is there a serpent lurking in the Connerys' garden?

Luciana Paluzzi brought the wisdom of the Italian female to bear on that subject. She had no doubts. 'Can't you see they are very much in love?' she sighed. 'If they were not they wouldn't care enough to have fights.'

If, indeed, there was a serpent it could only have been in the character of James Bond because Diane Cilento saw very little of Connery from the day she arrived. He was at work from six in the morning either swimming under the sea, flying high and low in a helicopter, or being chased by assorted villains through the streets and on the beaches of Nassau. When he did get back to the bungalow he could not relax because he had to study the script and discuss plans for the next day's shooting.

While she stretched out for a suntan in the Garden of Eden, her husband as Bond was making love with the ambitious Miss Auger deep down under the brilliant blue waters of the Atlantic. And, as one observer was quick to point out, although Mr Bond had made an instant impact on many women, this was the first time he had felt such a compelling affection while wearing an oxygen mask.

As Miss Auguer put it: 'The Bond women are the women of the nuclear age: they are free, and they make love when they want to without worrying about it afterwards. In this film we have this love scene underwater – for the first time in a movie, I think. We have our breathing equipment and we go down and down and down, right to the sandy bottom. And then the top of my bikini floats to the surface. It is very novel, don't you think?'

The word novel held an entirely different meaning for Diane Cilento at this period in her life. She had tried to relax with the children, cooking, swimming and playing golf, but with no one to share her innermost thoughts she became bored beyond belief. So she decided to put her thoughts on paper and began to write her first book, a novel she called *The Manipulator*. It was a candid insight into the lives and loves and behind-the-scenes scheming of a bunch of film moguls and their women at a Mexican film festival. Curiously and perhaps coincidentally, her husband's last film, *The*

Hill, was the British entry for the Cannes Film Festival that year.

She explained how she felt. 'This industry can take hold of you and wrap you up like a piece of meat and then you are left with about 20 per cent of your time for yourself and your family. It is not enough. Neither Sean nor I mean to allow ourselves to be packaged by this business. We will not allow ourselves to become that involved.

'I am through the other side of being Mrs James Bond, and although it still happens, it cannot upset me any longer. Sean and I have our lives to lead in our own way. Strangely enough, perhaps, I am not too ambitious any more, I am not caught up. I have my children and my home and I shall work when it is right and only then. But we are not going to let ourselves be merchandized.'

They were brave words in view of the fact that all around her were teams of reporters and photographers sent out to the West Indies by newspapers and magazines from almost every nation in the world to capture Bond and his exploits which had inflamed the Vatican (its paper *Osservatore Romano* attacked him for 'vulgarity, sex and sadism'), infuriated Moscow (who regarded him as an enemy and a tool of Western intelligence), and shocked the Salvation Army ('cruelty for the love of cruelty' bellowed *War Cry*).

'It was a madhouse out there,' says Tom Carlisle, the publicist. 'I don't think anyone confronted with such blinding limelight and exposure to the world's media could possibly cope with it.'

For most of it Sean Connery felt boredom and contempt, which he did his best to stifle. When a languid lady at a society party in Nassau came up and said, 'With all this success as Bond do you think you'll ever be able to do anything else?' he turned away.

What he could not turn away from, however determined he and his wife were to remain detached from it, was the ever-spiralling success of the Bond films themselves. Even as he made underwater love with the aid of oxygen, the accountants were entering another rarefield atmosphere, computing that the three Bond films he had made so far were then earning at the rate of £1,000 an hour. Every hour. Day and night. A round-the-clock £24,000. That was the financial measure of his personal success as 007 according to the book-keepers.

Even as *Goldfinger* was showing with the belting voice of Shirley Bassey soaring over the title as a theme song, they had re-issued *Dr No* and *From Russia With Love* as a double bill in America, and the films were proving the best three trailers in the business for the film he was making now. The takings from the three already totalled £23 million, which meant a net profit of at least £10 million to the makers, with the cash registers relentlessly clicking on.

Could he walk away from that? Well, he could walk away from Bond, he thought, but not from the money. As he said: 'I am concerned about the money I earn from the films because I think I should get every penny I am entitled to. In fact, I want every damn penny I can get. I've given my pound of flesh for it.'

At this point he knew that there was no more he could get out of Bond as an actor and he thought there must be something else he could do that would involve him with people other than shooting, throttling, stabbing and burying them. As he said on Love Beach before taking a final swim and going off to cook himself eggs and bacon: 'Out here you live like a gangster, don't you? I mean, champagne, yachts and fast cars. Like it was all going to end tomorrow.'

But he knew it would not be ending tomorrow. According to his contract he had two more Bond films to make. After that, if they wanted him to do more, it would be $1 million he would ask for and 10 per cent of the gross.

That summer, back in England for June and the finish of *Thunderball*, he devoted himself to playing as much golf as he could, sometimes with his wife but more often with *aficionados* of the game such as Bruce Forsyth and Ronnie Carroll. Comedians and singers, it seems, took more readily to golf, or maybe, because of their lifestyles which dictated working mostly at night, had more time for it during the day than gainfully employed actors. Moreover, when you played for £50 or £100 a corner it tended to concentrate the mind wonderfully.

Surprisingly for a Scot Connery had come late to the game, having been introduced to it by Robert Shaw during the filming of *From Russia With Love* in Istanbul on a course they both described as diabolical. However, his real interest and passion for golf had developed as a result of that duel with Goldfinger at 'Royal St Mark's' played out at Stoke Poges. For that he had had to practise hard and take lessons from the pros in order that his swing lent a passable resemblance to a nine handicap player, even though the results of his strokes needed special camera work to hide the truth.

Now his approach was altogether more convincing and his game revealed much of what Bond's creator Iam Fleming, who himself had been a keen golfer, had in mind; a strong, fullish swing, an enjoyment of competition and an obvious flair for a devastating shot, particularly near the green.

'If I could be a scratch golfer,' Connery said at this stage, 'I'd take six months off a year and go on the pro circuit. No, really, I mean it.'

Late that June he played in the pro-amateur Bowmaker tournament at Sunningdale where some of his shots would have produced sinister chuckles from Goldfinger, especially when he carved a drive so deep into jungle country the ball was never seen again. Nevertheless, his partners, the South African star Coble Le Grange and the 1961 English champion Ian Caldwell, conceded that he was improving.

In August he holidayed with *Thunderball* producer Terence Young in the south of France where *Goldfinger* was showing. He stood for fifteen minutes in front of a poster announcing the film and no one recognized him. He was pleased. What of the image now?

It was too soon for him to be complacent. The merchandizing of Bond had begun to create a Frankenstein monster. In October, when he was filming another get-away-from-Bond picture *A Fine Madness* in Hollywood, he took time out to play in a pro-am golf tournament in Las Vegas. There he learned that souvenir piracy in America, including Bond shirts, underwear, guns and dolls with spikes that came out of their shoes, was costing something like £140,000 a year just to fight.

Legitimate merchandizing had already begun on an international scale. In America alone $62 million worth was put out by the Licensing Corporation of America. There were James Bond cosmetics, gift-wrapped 007 aftershave, suits, socks, games and toys – and all of it hit the markets for Christmas 1965 when *Thunderball* burst on the public.

Sean Connery and his wife were sitting quietly at home when the film was premiered in London. They didn't go because they had seen the film privately in Hollywood the week before.

In the early hours of the morning after the crowds had gone home it was discovered that all eight pictures of Connery as James Bond – all of them large-scale scenes from the film – had been unscrewed from their frames outside the cinema and spirited away. 'Such a thing hasn't happened since the Beatles,' said the manager.

Bondmania had arrived.

12

A Time for Change

In the American bar of the Dorchester Hotel in London's Park Lane, Kevin McClory, the Irishman who had rowed himself into the Saltzman-Broccoli partnership for *Thunderball*, was button-holing an Irish senator and pulling sheaves of box-office returns for the film that had just come in from the United States. To say that he was aglow would be an understatement.

'Look,' he said to me, turning to order ten cases of Dom Perignon for delivery to his home as another man might request a modest gin and tonic, 'have a look at these. Did you know that this film has already taken $1,130,000 in one week alone in New York? In some world centres it's topping *Goldfinger* by as much as 49 per cent.'

'And you on 2½ per cent,' I said.

'You must be kidding,' he replied. 'Multiply that by ten and you might be nearer the mark. Seriously, it's doing fantastic business. I was in Tokyo with Cubby, and the cinema was so packed you couldn't have got another single person inside it. The manager of the place was nearly in tears, though, because it was winter and not summer. He said he could have got another 100 people in if it hadn't been for their overcoats.'

McClory is something of a joker in full flood and he looked as though he had kissed the Blarney Stone when he told me how he and Cubby Broccoli had broken the bank at Macao. 'At one stage we were flat broke, y'see. We tried to raise credit but they wouldn't let us have any. Cubby was desperate. "I'll give you the next week's takings from *Goldfinger*," he told them. But they wouldn't have it. Finally we got a film company executive to wake up his bank manager with an IOU. He came back with the money and we went on to break the bank with it. I slept with my money in $100 bills under my bed that night.'

This was the way of it, part of the crazy euphoria generated by Bondmania. They'd taken over the ghost of the Paramount theatre on New York's Broadway, refurbished it to take 2,000 paying customers and played the film twenty-four hours round the clock. Not only that. They had the money from the popcorn sales, too, and at 3 a.m. the place looked as though a circus had hit town.

Sean Connery did not begrudge others their fun where they could find it and he felt no guilt about the films seeing him well on the way to becoming a millionaire. What irked this man of basically simple tastes was the whole Bond bonanza which packaged and marketed his talent, his time, sweat and effort. With the kind of money now involved it was beginning to verge on the obscene, and he still felt he was not getting his fair share from those who were living off his back. As he says, 'If the terms had been more generous, it could have been a different story.'

And as Denis Selinger says: 'Sean has always felt this way about the rewards for his work. If he has a million he's always thinking it should be a million and a half – and not without reason. Sean has taken some bad financial knocks in his time from so-called advisers and there have been cases where the book-keeping has not always been as it should be.'

Without the aid of *Thunderball*, which grossed $28 million in America alone (and that was only the first time out), Sean Connery was named the most popular star with British cinemagoers for the second year in succession. According to the *Motion Picture Herald* he did it purely on the re-issue of *Dr No* and *From Russia With Love*, and his out-of-Bond appearance in *The Hill*. Their survey placed him way ahead of Elvis Presley, Julie Andrews, Sophia Loren, Rex Harrison, the Beatles, Richard Burton, Peter Sellers, Peter O'Toole and John Wayne.

He was now in the process of re-negotiating his contract with Broccoli and Saltzman and if he didn't reach an agreement on percentage terms he would not be available for the fifth Bond film on the drawing-board, *You Only Live Twice*. At the same time he let it be known that he planned to return to the theatre at the end of the year, but this time as a director. He would direct a play called *The Secret of the World*, written by Ted Allan Herman, which had been first staged in Britain at Stratford East but had never reached the West End. He planned to stage it in New York with Shelley Winters as the star.

He explained his decision. He was now thirty-five and when he had reached his thirty-fifth birthday the previous year he had felt a significant change in himself and his attitudes. 'I suddenly realized that I was half-way there. And I found that because of that realization I felt younger. I discovered I was choosing brighter colours for my clothes. I was heavier, too. I weighed fifteen stone compared with the year before when I was fourteen stone five. And I promised myself that from now on and for the next thirty-five years I would do only the things that excited me. That's why I want to direct my first play in New York. Of course a lot of people say it's madness, that when thirty-eight out of forty-four new productions have flopped on Broadway in the past season it's hardly the time for an untried English director to be welcomed there. But I'm going because I like the play and I want to do it.'

He reckoned that if you did not enjoy at least 60 per cent of the work you chose to do then life became monotonous and routine. Money was something else. 'One doesn't do everything for money, but one should be paid what one is worth. In the past couple of years I could have made several million dollars if I had taken on a tame manager to promote me in connection with golf balls or whisky or something like that. But I don't want to sell myself like that.

'My reason for wanting the money I think I'm entitled to is simple. Money gives you the freedom and power to do what you want. I want to use the power I have now to be a producer. Not one who merely has some notepaper with his name on the top, but a real one using his power the way Taylor and Burton do to get things done that they want to do. What I'm tired of is a lot of fat slob producers living off the backs of lean actors.'

However, much as he admired the financial clout that gave stars like Burton and Taylor their artistic freedom, he also knew he was a loner. Unlike the Burtons, who moved around with a near-regal caravanserai of retainers, advisers, agents, fixers, managers, wheeler-dealers, lawyers, dogsbodies and hangers-on, he had learned to rely on himself since he was nine and out earning a crust to help support the family. 'I make my own decisions, maybe discuss them with Diane and then pass them on to my lawyer, agent and accountant. That's the only way to breathe,' he said.

The air he found sweetest to breathe was on the golf course, and in the spring and early summer of 1966, when Diane Cilento was in the United States to make the film *Hombre* with Paul Newman,

taking along the children and the unfinished manuscript of the book
she was writing about fat slob producers, he was out with friends
like Michael Medwin, Eric Sykes and Bruce Forsyth. They toured
the famous Guinness brewery on the banks of the Liffey on a golfing
holiday in Dublin, and in the Isle of Man Connery mixed golf with
pleasure and business when he opened a new casino there. Roulette
was not his game. He preferred chemmy and poker and played in a
private room with a select few.

He played golf hard and continuously. He now had a handicap of
fourteen and considered himself a good match player but not a good
stroke player when he was alone. Almost as though to prove his
point, he blasted his way to second place in the better ball section of
Sir Billy Butlin's pro-am stroke tournament on a wind-lashed
course at Carnoustie in early June.

But it was his off-the-course activities that fascinated many, not
least the actress Miss Diana Dors. 'After a day's golf at Wentworth,
people like Ronnie Carroll, Bruce Forsyth, Eric Sykes, Stanley Baker
and Sean Connery would gather at my house and play Truth or
Consequences. One would be chosen to sit in the middle of the
room, which was known as the Hot Seat, and the others would be
allowed to question him about any personal or provocative subject
they chose. Most of the questions, as you can imagine, were of a
sexual nature.

'For example, Ronnie Carroll once asked Ed "Kooky" Byrne,
then famous for his 77 *Sunset Strip* television series: "Have you ever
had an affair with a man?" From "Kooky" it produced the fast
answer: "Sure. Hasn't everybody?" Which, of course, had everyone
falling about.

'If the victim did not tell the truth or was discovered to be lying or
the general vote was against him, a forfeit had to be paid. Some of
the forfeits were ingenious, some cruel and others quite ghastly. I
won't go into details, but I've known marriages break up because of
the Hot Seat.'

As Dors says, the game was only amusing if you were on your
own minus wife, husband or lover, because the question, if asked,
could then be answered with complete freedom and to the delight of
questioners who were avid for intimate details of your private life.

And the one curious aspect she noted was that whenever someone
else was in the Hot Seat, it was Sean Connery who took charge of
the game. Unwilling to admit details of his own very private life in

public, he seemed obsessed with obtaining the truth, the whole truth and nothing but the truth from others.

'Judge Jeffreys had nothing on Sean,' says Dors. 'He was like a ringmaster, shouting instructions and abuse in his Scots accent to all concerned. Players had to adhere to the rules and tell the truth, for he was adamant that no one should be a hypocrite or ever dare hide the facts. To me, Sean was much more interested in extracting the truth from someone than in getting the victim to pay a penalty which, to the others, was the most amusing part of the game.

'He was at the height of his Bond fame and he could have had any woman in the world. As far as I could see he often did, because the girls flung themselves at him. He is a very natural, basic man. Sometimes he can be quite blunt and even hurtful in the things he says but you do know where you stand with him. He is no hypocrite and he doesn't suffer fools gladly.'

This was the year when a party of them went to the Big Fight at Harringay. This was the world heavyweight championship clash between Henry Cooper, Our 'Enery of Bellingham, Kent, and that colourful character who became Muhammed Ali but who, for better or verse (he was always talking in rhyme), was then Cassius Clay, otherwise known as the Louisville Lip.

As most of those in the party were celebrities who had paid around £50 apiece to witness the action, they were quickly beseiged by autograph hunters and were kept busily signing away until the lights went up. To roars of applause, Cassius Clay made his entrance to the ring. 'The air of excitement you could almost feel, see and touch,' says Dors. 'There was a blue haze of cigar smoke ringside and the crowd was tensed, keyed-up, as the bell went for the first round.

'I could see Sean hunched forward in his seat, intent on watching every move the fighters made. And then, half-way through the round, a woman came up with a book and shoved it under our noses. She completely blocked our view and unfortunately for her she thrust the book at Sean. I might have signed, but not Sean. Without too much restraint he snapped: 'Get out of my bloody way, woman. D'you think I've paid 50 quid a seat to sit here and look at *you*?'

In July 1966, in the week his film *A Fine Madness* opened in London to mixed reviews (he was playing a Beatnik poet), he was taking care of his bills on the eve of flying to Japan for *You Only*

Live Twice. There was a cheque made out to the Inland Revenue for £15,000 and other items totalling some £800. The trouble with cheques, he thought, was that you lost sight of the fact that it was money. As he said: 'Now, if you had to pay it all out in notes you would soon see what it all meant.'

He felt that this was a time for change. He had put his rambling, elegant home at Acton on the market for £17,950, or a near offer, because he felt he was losing his privacy there. People had come to know the house and they would stand outside staring in at his wife and himself as they sat in the main room. If it had gone on he reckoned that one day he might be found guilty of assault. Furthermore, there were those who had not just stood outside but had stepped in to help themselves to jewellery and any other valuables they could find when he and his wife were away.

The next time he thought he might find somewhere in the centre of London, in Knightsbridge or Grosvenor Square, where they could be more anonymous and where, at the weekends, it was almost deserted, rather like a village.

He was not in a particularly good mood when he left London. The reviews of *A Fine Madness* in which he played with Joanne Woodward, Paul Newman's wife, had been good in New York but the London critics had found his performance hard-going. 'Sean Connery,' wrote Leonard Mosley in the *Daily Express*, 'crashes from scene to scene like a mixture of Brendan Behan and Dylan Thomas well pickled by the third bottle of the evening. But the boorish behaviour lacks the compensation which made Behan-Thomas tolerable to their friends even in their worst moments – the sense of imagery, the power with words, the artistic vision, the fact that they were poets.

'In this film Connery not only looks like a clod. He is a clod. And that means he isn't funny. Or touching either.

'If he wants to be funny, let him stick to the Bond films and play the fantasies straight. We will do the laughing.'

It was the kind of review which must have caused great glee in the Broccoli-Saltzman camp, but set Connery's teeth on edge because he had thought the film well worth doing. 'A film when it is finished is like a young bird leaving the nest. It can be shot down, but if you believed in it in the first place then it doesn't matter.'

When he flew into Bangkok he said that *You Only Live Twice* would be his last film as Bond.

13

You Only Live Twice

That most journeyed journalist of our times, Mr Alan Whicker, could hardly credit even his experienced, quizzical eyes behind the famous horn-rimmed glasses. That he had the edge on most of the world's press corps who were congregating in Tokyo for the latest Bond epic he had no doubt. Wherever he went these days Mr Whicker was a privileged observer, fronting as he did television programmes which regularly pulled in something like fifteen million viewers.

The lobbies of the Tokyo Hilton were thick with jostling Japanese *papparazzi*, highly persistent mobs of small, darting men who were made to look even smaller by their telephoto lenses which dangled from their camera slings like sub-machine guns between their knees, almost dragging them to the ground. But these photographers could be even more waspish than their Roman counterparts along the Via Veneto. For one thing, they had better cameras.

Sean Connery had arrived in Tokyo with his wife Diane Cilento by a circuitous route, having left Bangkok under pressure of crowd worship and Manila pursued by Filipino fans. They had avoided Hong Kong for fear of what might happen to them in that teeming city and had been successfully smuggled into Japan in a secret undercover operation. As Diane Cilento remarked, it was a fantastic lifestyle.

By the next morning, when word spread that Bondo-san was in town, the hotel was under siege by photographers, but Sean Connery, on his first visit to Japan and with only one night in Tokyo before flying south to begin filming, wanted to see some life before he left. This task was vouchsafed to the amiable Cubby Broccoli, who revelled in his considerable powers to organize such a clandestine exercise.

Which is why Alan Whicker found himself tip-toeing from Cubby's suite (what else would it be but 1007?) that night for a secret expedition into the brightest Ginza. With the hotel lobby carpeted wall-to-wall with expectant cameramen, Whicker and Cubby and Sean Connery and his wife took the service lift to an underground garage where two limousines waited, their engines smoothly purring.

Watched only by a few giggling girls from the massage rooms, Sean and Diane went into one limousine, says Whicker, and he and Cubby into the other. And off they sped down a backstreet heading flat-out for the sukiyaki. Before they had travelled more than fifty yards they discovered that five waiting cars, each of them crammed with cameramen, had spotted them and were roaring in pursuit, telephoto lenses sticking out of the windows like tommy-guns in an old Capone movie.

'We raced through the night streets,' relates Whicker, 'tyres squealing, hearts racing. I was petrified, but to the chauffeurs it was nothing because they always drive like that. When we reached the restaurant we bolted through a fusillade of flashbulbs while Cubby organized defence-in-depth at the door.

'Around about crab-salad time things quietened down a bit. And then, as we were about to tackle those giant Kobe steaks – the ones that lie sizzling across broad platters with one end hanging on the floor – someone shouted: "Look out! There's one!" A man who had been passing himself off as a casual bar-fly suddenly showed himself in his true flashlight. He grabbed a couple of frantic pictures and fled pursued by waiters.

'The small, slim woman who owned the place leapt across to cut him off and there were sounds of a struggle behind the door. We all flinched but she must have known something about judo. When she reappeared this little woman was carrying the man's camera. And then another kamikaze cameraman went into action.

'A Japanese gent who had been sipping his *sake* at the next table suddenly transmogrified before our very eyes into a frenzied photographer – and the lady of the house went after him, too. There were crashing and bumping sounds and this time she returned triumphant bearing a wristwatch. It later turned out that it belonged to her own barman, who should have kept his arm out of her business, but it shows you how she was in there grabbing way.'

Whicker's account of the evening's Oriental shennanigans is

important because it accurately describes the kind of exposure which pressurized Sean Connery and completely soured his relationship with Japanese photographers. His frustration and anger not unnaturally spread to any journalist sent to cover the latest Bond story. And they came by the plane-load.

There was no escape from the fearful zoom lens. Not even in the most private places. Stanley Sopel says: 'What happened during the making of that picture was absolutely unbelievable. Sean couldn't even go to the lavatory without these Japanese shoving Nikkons up his arse. And I mean that quite literally. They actually tried to picture him over the top of toilet room doors.'

The following morning Cubby Broccoli arranged for a press reception in the ballroom of the Tokyo Hilton and there were more than 500 in the room. Sean Connery came on stage casually dressed in shirt and jeans and the first question was: 'Why are you, Mr James Bond, dressed like that?' That was almost the end of the conference. He exploded like a flashbulb himself. 'I'm here for your bloody convenience and I can dress any way I damn well want.'

Questions that made the Bond entourage wince because of their stunning banality followed:

'After your experience in Bond films, will you start a private detective agency?'

'No.'

'What do you do when your children misbehave?'

'I beat them.'

'What is tattooed on your arm?'

'Scotland Forever and Mum and Dad.'

'Why aren't you wearing a tie?'

'Why aren't you?'

For almost two hours Connery burned as these trivialities were solemnly translated back and forth as though they were pearls of ultimate wisdom, and when the stories were printed the next day one headline read: JAMES BOND WANTS TO EAT RAW FISH.

The location was a rough one. A mosquito-ridden spot called Ibusuki on the farthest south-west tip of the southernmost main island of Kyushu. The coolest place was the water and at this point the East China Sea was like warm syrup. Here, standing on the flimsy wooden jetty that pierced the blue-green bay like a splintered pencil, it was like sweltering in a Turkish bath. A shade temperature of 96 degrees with 85 per cent humidity. Even as Sean Connery cradled another can of ice-cold beer in his massive fist he knew that if he did not drink it in ten minutes it would be warm as toast and that when he had drunk it the beer would take only another ten minutes to ooze from every pore of his tanned body as perspiration. Still, the five minutes of momentary pleasure in slaking his thirst was worth the extra sweat and discomfort it would bring later.

He was scarcely recognizable, wearing a specially-woven Beatle-type wig fringed like a shorn-off coconut on top of his balding head. His face had been darkened by make-up, his eyes narrowed to slits, and he was wearing a loose-fitting blue smock shirt and baggy trousers, his big feet encased in open, rough-hewn sandals.

Disguised as a deaf-and-dumb Japanese fisherman, he nevertheless towered like Gulliver above the Lilliputian photographers whose cameras constantly clicked away like a million frantic grasshoppers. Every time he moved, fifty cameramen moved too, like a reflex action. 'They've followed me into the bloody lavatory again,' he bellowed in a voice that sent the pack scurrying back to their hideouts. 'They've been coming at me like a firing squad!'

In the shelter of the only inn this tiny fishing village of Akime could boast, taken over and dubbed 'The Inn of the 007th Happiness' by the ninety-six-strong film unit, he flopped into a chair while a make-up expert checked his features. 'No more,' he said. 'This one's the last. Frankenstein's taken over.' He turned his face to a cooling stream of air from a portable electric fan. 'I admit Bond has done more for me probably than any character has done for an actor in history and I'm not ungrateful for that. But think how it feels – every day the same questions. For *four years*. Tell me: how would you feel?'

Outside, dragonflies measuring all of six inches were performing lazy aerobatics in the stifling heat and there were cockroaches of a similar giant size scuttling obscenely across grey lava rocks. At the back of the village a landing strip had been built to accommodate the orange twenty-five-seater helicopter that daily transported the entire unit away from this horrendous spot to their hotels in Ibusuki, ten minutes' flying time away.

Lewis Gilbert, a quietly-spoken veteran film director, was in charge of *You Only Live Twice* and the script bore little resemblance to Ian Fleming's rather dull travelogue of Japan which made up his eleventh book on the super-spy who had captured the imagination of an entire generation. Cubby Broccoli and Harry Saltzman had invested something like £2·5 million for what the wags on location were calling Connery's epic-taph and had brought in that top teller of tales of the unexpected, Roald Dahl, to write the screenplay.

'I think we're going to pull it off,' said Gilbert who had done his energetic best to appease Connery's outrage at all the irritants on this location, including an injection against encephalitis, the sleeping sickness that could be caused by the native mosquitoes. 'The fact is that apart from a pitched battle in a volcano and a Russian space project, there aren't too many gimmicks in this one. We've tried to make Bond more human. To let audiences see that he suffers more when things happen.'

Connery, who was feeling somewhat less than human that day, said in tones of silken irony: 'That's right. We make him care. When one of my girlfriends gets shot I am allowed to show some emotion. Not too much, mind. But some.'

In the evenings, away from the location and with the nearest golf course some 500 miles away, Connery played table-tennis with his wife or sat with her in their room talking with the unit's top brass and not always about the next day's shooting.

'They were always kind and considerate to me,' says Stanley Sopel. 'I occupied the room next to theirs and every time I got back to the hotel exhausted from the heat and conditions there would be a knock on the adjoining wall. "I think you need a drink," Sean would say. I'd go in and join them and there was not only a drink waiting for me but intelligent conversation, which I found stimulating and refreshing. Diane was well-read, witty and much more intelligent than the average bird you find in our business and she had this strong physical attraction to go with it. It was obvious Sean adored her being there. In fact everyone in the unit did.'

When Diane Cilento returned to England and the family home in Acton, which was now on the market, she almost immediately wished she had not. Sean Connery was still in Japan when a burglar broke into the house, smashing his way through a door panel, and proceeded to go berserk. Trophies were shattered, ink spattered about, curtains torn down, souvenirs, tape recorders and television sets smashed. Pictures were pulled from the walls and shelves ripped away. Even the contents of the refrigerator had been thrown out on to the floor.

It was the fifth break-in since they had moved into the house, but this kind of vandalism they had not known before. Alerted to the dangers his wife and their two children were faced with, Sean Connery demanded immediate protection, at least until he returned from Tokyo. A security firm manned by three former Metropolitan police officers was brought in and from then on the Connery home was guarded by a security patrolman and an Alsatian dog throughout the night.

The penalties attached to being Agent 007 had now reached a stage where his family was not merely involved with the outside world he tried to keep at bay. They were placed at considerable physical risk. There was the fear that any screwball could walk in at will at any time and wreak havoc and maybe worse. Here was another reason why he was glad to be freed of the Bond shackles, however gold-plated. Broccoli and Saltzman had agreed to release him from the sixth Bond picture he was due to make under the terms of his contract. They had done it provided he worked for them in Japan for his agreed contract price as it had been amended and a share of the profits. Which meant that he would walk away with £50,000 plus an agreed rate on overtime plus a percentage if the film did well. In fact, he earned £170,000 in overtime alone on that picture.

There had been a lot of greed around. Everyone connected with the Bond industry had made enough money by this time to live for ever in comfort until they buried themselves and their families.

From now on he put a price on his own head. Anyone who wanted Sean Connery for a film would be made aware that the going rate for his services would be $200,000 per film plus 5 per cent of the takings, or $400,000 a film if he forfeited his percentage.

This made him one of the highest-paid actors in the world, if not the highest at that time. Maybe he could now sort out the future so that his filming fitted in with his golf rather than the other way round.

14

The Bowler and the Bunnet

Over the years there had been many attempts to cash in on the Bond industry in terms of spin-offs, rip-offs and copycat movies which attempted a similar spy formula. But none of them annoyed and disgusted Connery quite so much as the blatant attempt to cash in on his brother.

Early in 1966 his younger brother Neil, a plasterer by trade before he became a photographer of weddings and christenings in Edinburgh, had been flown to Rome in secret to take some film tests. He was wearing one of the immaculate Savile Row tailored suits given to him by Sean, who always inherited the entire Bond wardrobe – some fifteen or twenty suits and a collection of hand-made shirts, some from Lanvin Paris – at the end of a Bond picture. Only the trousers had to be shortened for Neil because Sean was taller.

Now, as the year was coming to a close, Neil Connery found himself aboard a white-hulled, three-masted schooner as it sailed into Monte Carlo harbour from the Mediterranean, and with him was what looked suspiciously like an all-Bond cast. There was Daniela Bianchi (Bond's sleeping partner in *From Russia With Love*), Adolfo Celi (the villain in *Thunderball*), the Canadian actress Lois Maxwell and Britain's Bernard Lee, who were Miss Moneypenny and 'M' in all the Bond films. Also aboard was a young actor who called himself Gydo Lollobrigida.

They were all taking part in an Italian picture which was an obvious and candid attempt to cut into the handsome profits harvested by the Bond image, because the unabashed title of the movie they planned to show around the world was *Operation Kid Brother*.

Sean Connery tried to stop the film. He told the director, one

Dorio Sabetello: 'By getting my brother to make this kind of picture you are exploiting us both.'

At least, those were the only words he used which are fit to print. In his book here was another fat slob film-maker trying to turn some Italian lire into a fast American buck by muscling in on territory which he had made his own.

James Bond was not mentioned by name in the film, but snatches of bedroom dialogue leaked out. There was Daniela Bianchi telling Neil, who was playing a famous plastic surgeon persuaded by the British Government to undertake a Secret Service mission: 'Your brother was never like this.' And Lois Maxwell breathing: 'If you were in the Secret Service for long you would kill your brother's reputation both as an agent and as a bedmate.'

Neil was embarrassed when it became known he was the second Bond to get into the act. 'Sean was only trying to protect me,' he said. 'As brothers we are close and always will be. The feud isn't between us. Sean is not so much worried about what has happened to me as the way in which it has happened. In any case, Dorio talked at the wrong time.'

For sheer, bare-faced cheek Signor Dorio Sabetello was hard to beat. A rhinocerous would have been thin-skinned by comparison. He even asked Sean Connery if he would pose with his brother for a publicity picture to help promote the film. He was not just abruptly turned down. Sean Connery hit the roof without the aid of an ejector seat or any other sophisticated item of the Bond gadgetry.

Signor Sabetello just went on grinning and went so far as to suggest that Neil could, if his brother was abdicating, take over future James Bond roles. To which Harry Saltzman when he heard replied: 'One thing is certain. Neil Connery will never take over from his brother as James Bond.'

Neil Connery, who was collecting rather less than £5,000 for his part in the picture and had already collected five stitches in his leg as the result of a fall on the schooner's deck, denied he was being taken for a ride on his brother's back. 'You may think I'm trying to cash in on my brother's scene,' he said, 'but I can tell you he's sick to death of playing James Bond.'

And so he was.

Strangely for a man who had never once bothered to cast a vote in his life, Sean Connery now began to take an active interest in social and political issues. Maybe he was developing a social conscience as an antidote to becoming what he called a fat slob producer himself now that both he and his wife were wealthy beyond the dreams of avarice, with tax-haven companies registered in the Bahamas and she owning several miles of coastline in her native Queensland, Australia. Maybe it had something to do with the fact that he had promised himself that from now on he would do only those things that excited him intellectually. And maybe it had something to do with him being Scottish, which he considered the greatest virtue of all.

'The Scots have nothing in common with the English,' he said then. 'The Scots are Scottish. Period. So it's useless for them to compare me with James Bond. Bond is English and I'm Scottish. And I don't like the English at all because I am Scottish. Period. I only get angry when they ask me if I'd like to be James Bond, if I'm like James Bond, if they should call me Connery or Bond, when they plague me with idiocies of that kind: not when they make me talk about Bond.

'Why should I? The Bond films are amusing, each one is more exacting than the last, each one is of a better quality than the last. And I'll tell you: if I hadn't acted Shakespeare, Pirandello, Euripides – in short, what is classed as serious theatre, I should never have managed to play James Bond. It's not so easy, that role.

'Frankly, it was all luck. And luck only knocks once. And when it knocks you have to grab it quick and then hang on tight.'

He had hung on tight. For the third year running he had topped the popularity poll in Britain's cinemas with *Thunderball*, which had then taken more than £1,250,000 at the box office. And now he had his independence. As 1967 dawned he made his first venture into theatre management. He was with the angels at last. Excited by the Oxford Playhouse production of Ben Jonson's *Volpone* with Leo McKern (the actor who was to become a television triumph in later years as Rumpole of the Bailey) and Leonard Rossiter (yet to achieve fame in *Rising Damp* and those television commercials wherein he dampened the lap of Miss Joan Collins), he teamed up with impresario Peter Bridge to bring it to the West End for a six-week season at the Garrick theatre in London.

When a £50,000 plan was announced to convert a London Methodist hall into a modern theatre and Britain's first fully-equipped training centre for actors and directors, Connery was among the patrons who launched a national appeal with Lord Harewood and the Duchess of Bedford. In conjunction with several universities they wanted to encourage the work of literary translation by setting up a panel of translators and, as a result, bring to the stage many neglected works which could be considered by the managements of the great national companies and of theatres throughout Britain. In all this was sensed the desires of his wife Diane Cilento. But in March 1967 Sean Connery came into his own.

That was the month he chose to make his first move on the political scene when he came out on the side of the Scottish Nationalists by sending a letter and a photograph for political use to George Leslie, a veterinary surgeon fighting for the Nationalist cause in Pollok, Glasgow, in a by-election. He wrote: 'I am convinced that with our resources and skills we are more than capable of building a vigorous and modern self-governing Scotland in which we can all take pride and which will deserve the respect of other nations.'

What this meant was that he actively supported Mr Leslie's proposition of a Customs border along the Cheviots, separate Scots armed forces, a separate Parliament in Edinburgh and separate negotiations for the Common Market. His new-found determination to strike a blow for Scotland whenever and wherever he could was no longer in doubt. And it was to be reinforced in the coming weeks.

At a golfing society dinner in London Sean Connery met Sir Iain Stewart, a former deputy chairman of Scottish Television who had been a successful but comparatively unknown Scottish industrialist until he became responsible for what was known as the Fairfields experiment. This was a much troubled shipyard on the Clyde in which the Government, the unions and private enterprise had jointly invested.

Stewart and Connery shared a dedication to golf but they had little else in common other than that both were Scots. Even then, as Connery pointed out, he was from Edinburgh and Stewart was from Glasgow and sons of these cities could be as far apart in terms of fraternal love as citizens of Dacca and Karachi.

Furthermore, Stewart was what Connery called 'a boss's son', educated with privilege at Loretto and Oxford, whereas Connery was a worker's son who had been enrolled only in the university of harsh and earnest life. So Connery's initial interest in Stewart's experiment in labour-management relations at Fairfields may not have been much more than sentimental loyalty to his working-class origins, but after several talks with Stewart in London he accepted an invitation to go up to Glasgow to see for himself.

What he saw excited him so much that he offered to make a documentary film about it and contribute his services free. The film was called *The Bowler and the Bunnet*. The 'bunnet', for the uninitiated, is the Lowland Scots equivalent of a cloth cap, sometimes, due to certain hazards in Glasgow, worn with a reinforced lining. And to Sean Connery this short documentary was as big a milestone in his life and times as an actor, trade unionist and expatriate Scot, as all the Bond films put together.

He said: 'With my background I know a bit about trade unions and all the problems, and what made me want to do the film in the first place was that Stewart was doing something at Fairfields that hadn't been done so successfully anywhere in the country, England included. He was bridging that terrible gulf between the bosses and the workers and he was breaking down the petty suspicions between unions. He even had carpenters doing painters' work when necessary and he had union men sitting in the boardroom. It was all working famously and production was going up. It was something to shout about.'

Connery endeared himself to the workers in Scotland. As one of them, a 44-year-old shop steward describes it: 'Sean made it clear from the outset that he was no toffee-nosed prima donna from London. He was every inch the Scotsman. He came down to our local pub, the Rob Roy in Govan Road, for a pint and he saw our trade union point of view. He was highly impressed when we told him that since the new regime at Fairfields the number of disputes had dropped by 70 per cent.'

Connery says: 'What that documentary film did for me in personal terms was to make me realize that part of me belonged to that kind of background. I thought I'd left it all behind me. I thought I'd been liberated from that claustrophobic John Knoxian narrow environment. Well, I had in a way because of the lifestyle connected with the Bond films, but I knew I just couldn't turn my back on it completely.'

It was during the making of that forty-minute documentary about industrial relations on Clydeside that the seeds of an idea for a

Scottish International Education Trust were planted, a project that was to become one of his major concerns. But he was bitter about the fate of the film. It was shown on Scottish Television but not networked. 'I offered it free to the B.B.C. and I.T.V, who turned it down,' he says. 'Too many important people came out of it badly. They say there's no political censorship in Britain, but there jolly well is. Things go on just the same and politics is all a question of money in the end. Ideologies leave me cold. Politicians go on talking about what they're going to do and I've never liked people who just talk.

'I like people who get on with things and do them well and do them thoroughly without making speeches. I'm a practical man.'

For a thriving capitalist he remained staunchly sympathetic to the workers and because he felt the way he did about Scotland he leaned increasingly towards Scottish Nationalism. He sincerely believed, as a practical man, that the Scots should have more control over their destiny as a nation. 'Over the centuries the Scots have accepted the fact of English domination,' he explained. 'You've only got to look at the figures to realize Scotland is a perpetually depressed area. Why else do the Scots have to leave Scotland to make a good living?'

He was talking in the days before the oil boom, but he was right when he said that Scotland was a divided nation so far as its people were concerned. In Scotland there were the stayers and the movers. He was glad he'd been one of the movers. And he kept on the move.

He moved from his house at Acton Park, so often beseiged by fans and penetrated by burglars. The refurbished Victorian convent in which he and Diane had been living was sold for £15,000 to a couple who turned it into a meditation centre propounding peace and spiritual sanctuary. Incense replaced Sean Connery's cigar smoke, vegetarian dishes supplanted steak, and exhortations to goodliness were arrayed on the walls.

The Connerys moved to Putney, where in May 1967 flowers were specially flown in from Acapulco in Mexico for a party arranged by Diane Cilento's publishers to promote the novel she had begun in the Bahamas and was now due for publication.

She was now working on her second novel, which revolved around a crooked land-developer in the West Indies. 'You become obsessed with your characters,' she said. 'You start to think about them while you're in the bath or driving the car and wondering how they might react in a given situation. When I finished my first book I felt a void. I had no more characters to think about, so I started a new one. I'm sure I've got to learn a lot about writing. But I know the more I write the more time I'll be able to spend at home.' She felt the need because young Jason Connery, who was then aged four, had become an amiable terror who only days before had smashed up a greenhouse with an axe.

Sean Connery supported his wife in her writing efforts. He had gone so far as to design the cover of *The Manipulators*, her first novel. It was a curious illustration, and he did not explain the symbolism. It was a surrealist picture of a man hanging upside down by his feet against an orange sunset. And for this he had been paid £30.

15

Looking for Something Different

A graphology expert was studying a specimen of Sean Connery's handwriting without knowing whose it was. He looked at the penmanship closely, evaluating the way certain letters were formed and from these he drew certain conclusions.

'This person's expectation of either their sexual or material gains has not been fulfilled,' he said. 'At least, not to their own satisfaction. Indeed it almost suggests that they don't particularly care because they are looking for something different.' There was a pause. He went on: 'The most significant part about the whole handwriting is that the actual connection between the letters is angular. Now an angular connection means a person who does not mind how much effort they have to put into what they think they need to achieve. To them the effort is nothing, but fulfilment is very necessary.

'The writing also suggests that this person is not of the hail-fellow-well-met type and does not go out of their way to please other people. This type does not kow-tow or crawl to anybody. It further suggests to me someone with a sense of purpose. When they start something there is a certain drop in their enthusiasm to begin with and then they gather strength increasing in enthusiasm until they become optimistic.

'I also see that they could be rather generous to old and trusted friends but not to new acquaintances.'

Shown the signature, the graphologist said: 'Ah. For everyone their signature is a rubber stamp they have been using all their life and is usually a little different from the rest of their handwriting. It is used to express and underline their personality. I do not know Sean Connery other than as a film star, of course, but from his signature both the shape of the "S" and the "C" suggest a lack of higher education. It reinforces my opinion that here is a purposeful man, one who is also highly sensual, and a man who doesn't care to a great extent if other people don't particularly like him.'

As a character reading of Sean Connery the man, the points made seemed uncannily accurate in that they were borne out by events in his personal history. It seemed strange to suggest that the man who had played James Bond should feel his sexual and material gains unfulfilled to his own satisfaction, but that he was looking for something different was obvious.

He began to grow his thinning hair long and in mid-June 1967 when he attended his first London premiere of a Bond film, *You Only Live Twice*, he was also sporting a Mexican-style moustache in preparation for a film he was to make with the French sex symbol Brigitte Bardot, a Western called *Shalako*.

It was a royal premiere and even the Queen was interested in why he did not want to play Bond any more. She asked him: 'Is this really your last Bond film?'

Connery replied: 'Yes, ma'am, I'm afraid it is.'

The Queen pressed on. 'Did you feel you were being typecast?'

Connery laughed. 'Yes, I think you are right, ma'am,' he said.

He was looking tanned and fit, having just returned from the sunshine of Marbella in southern Spain where he and Diane Cilento now had a villa adjacent to his fellow Scot and business mentor Sir Iain Stewart, with gardens leading to the first green of a golf course, and where they counted among their friends and neighbours Lew Hoad, the former Wimbledon tennis champion and his wife.

However, there was a disquieting note in some of the reviews of his performance in *You Only Live Twice*. 'Something has happened to Connery now that happens to all of us,' one critic wrote, 'and that is middle-age. But despite the thickening midriff, Bond still outstrips his imitators.' Months later, Connery would sue a French newspaper for suggesting that he was unfit to play Bond.

On the whole, the reviews were favourable, even enthusiastic, about his acting ability this time round, suggesting that instead of being a menu-reading thug he had risen to the suavity of a Cary Grant. 'Your daughter might not be safe with him,' observed one reviewer, 'but at least she'd be granted a decent burial . . . Connery is given a chance to reveal the appetite for life instead of a mere animal desire to get horizontal with the nearest available geisha. The slant-eyed maidens allotted to Connery are entirely appealing and one or two show a prudish eagerness to stay away from the mattress. In fact the innuendo of the film – and the entire cult depends on lascivious double-meaning – is far more subtle than before and Connery proves himself to be King Lear.'

Cary Grant *and* King Lear? This wasn't bad going for what he had decided was his swan song as Bond.

In July he shepherded his wife and their two children off on holiday to the south of France before proceeding to join his golf cronies for a junket to Belfast. Not even a family holiday was allowed to interfere with his golfing arrangements. This time the team included comic Charlie Drake, the comedians Eric Sykes and Les Dawson, and actors Stanley Baker and Michael Medwin. They were playing a team of Irish professionals including Christy O'Connor and Harry Bradshaw, and it would have taken a slick impresario a considerable amount of time and money to gather together these film and showbusiness types who played voluntarily in the name of charity. And fun.

Feeling considerably refreshed from this encounter he rejoined his family at Cap d'Antibes for the remainder of their Riviera holiday before going on to Deauville to meet Brigitte Bardot and her millionaire husband Gunther Sachs who, on being introduced to Connery for the first time, told him he would be accompanying Brigitte throughout the filming. Connery grinned. Gunther had a habit of sticking close as the ghost of Hamlet's father to his glamorous wife when she was filming opposite attractive leading men.

The Bond image lingered on in the public mind. In October, when he was once again nominated to be the rector of a Scottish university, this time St Andrews in Fife, a policeman served a speeding summons on Sean Connery. This was the third time it had happened in recent months but on this occasion the policeman's name happened to be Bond. James Bond.

When it became known that 007 Agent James Bond had been nicked by S21 Sergeant James Bond the hilarity in court was understandable.

The summons had been served on Sean Connery at a flat he had taken for the sake of convenience in Curzon Street, Mayfair, but he was away in Oslo at the time the case came up and the barrister representing him told the court solemnly: 'As you probably know, my client is a well-known actor who usually portrays a character called James Bond. And this case is not without its humorous side as the officer dealing with the case is also called James Bond. As you can imagine it has caused a certain amount of embarrassment to both parties.'

'I should think you are making history,' observed the magistrate drily.

As Sergeant James Bond said after giving evidence which resulted in a £15 fine for the other James Bond: 'I feel I'm unfortunate to have been born with the name but there's nothing I can do about it. Ever since this case arose I've been pestered out of my life by film and publicity men.'

The Bond image had also haunted Sean Connery in Oslo, where he had gone to see a psychiatrist. Was it becoming that serious, that he had to seek help at a psychiatric clinic? It was left to Diane Cilento to explain: 'Sean is not in hospital. Not in that sense. He had to go to Oslo to see friends and discuss some business. While he was there he decided to pay a visit to Dr Ola Rakne. He is a great admirer of his work and has read many of his books. He's certainly not unwell or having treatment of any kind.'

Dr Ola Rakne, who counted a number of film stars among the many patients he had from all parts of the world, was then aged eighty and the only surviving pupil of Dr Wilhelm Reich, a contemporary of Freud who claimed to be able to liberate people from their inhibitions through what he called vegeto-therapy. And if Sean Connery did have any inhibitions and was sharing them with Dr Rakne he was certainly not going to share them with the rest of the world. At his hotel he refused all calls.

A month later, when the result of the ballot for the office of rector of St Andrews' university was announced, Sean Connery came bottom of the list with 178 votes. The new rector of this Scottish hall of learning was to be Sir Learie Constantine, the former West Indies cricketer and barrister who went straight to the top of the list with 691.

There was some consolation for Connery when he was once again voted Britain's top box-office star of the year by America's *Motion Picture Herald*. It was becoming monotonous but it was also reassuring, and it was with this comforting thought that he flew off to welcome in the New Year in the warmth of Malaga.

*   *   *

It had taken producer Euan Lloyd three years to bring Sean Connery and Brigitte Bardot together and for the £2-million-budget film *Shalako* he had decided to show even the Americans how to make Westerns. When Connery had announced he would be exchanging his shoulder-holstered 7·65 mm Walther PPK for a low-slung ·45 Colt, hoots of derision could be heard all the way from Hollywood to Wardour Street because the history of motion pictures was littered with the graves of British actors who had tried to play cowboys. And Connery was the first ever Scottish cowboy to risk biting the dust.

Maybe that saved him, because the biggest man-trap for the British who sought to play cowboys was trying to impersonate the lazy drawl. Connery was able to use a softened version of his native Scottish burr and get away with it. As he said: 'It would have been a bad mistake to try a completely American accent. There were plenty of Scots immigrants in the West so I had no fear of being out of character.'

He played a frontier scout who rescued a party of European aristocrats from the Indians, among them Brigitte Bardot, a visiting French countess. And there was only one scene where a flash of the old Bond shone through. For most of the film he had to sweat, go unshaven, spit, sleep on straw, but then came the moment when he had to make amorous advances to his leading lady. There she was resisting him for fear of what the neighbours might say should they reach civilization again. With a leer he asked: 'Would it help if I said there was no hope of rescue?' It was pure 007, but the film confirmed that he could live down his Bond image and stay alive. It was pre-sold in thirty-six countries and recovered its production costs before a single public showing. And Connery could look forward to 30 per cent of the producer's profits. Filming of *Shalako* finished in early April 1968, and almost without a break he flew to Pennsylvania to begin making *The Molly Maguires* with Richard Harris, a film about tough miners in the 1870s, to confirm that he was free from the Bond straitjacket.

This was not been achieved without some friction. After he had made it plain that he was unwilling to continue that long-playing role one of the Bond film-makers was quoted in a French newspaper as saying that he had lost his sex appeal, developed a paunch and gone bald. Having worn a toupee for all the Bond films and having had his tailor confirm that he had not added one inch to his waistline, Connery sued the French paper – and won when the case finally came before the courts in 1969.

He received undisclosed libel damages and costs against *France-Soir*, which had asserted he was no longer fit to play the part of James Bond, thereby implying that he had not been honest when he had stated publicly that he was not undertaking further Bond roles because he did not wish to become typecast.

One curious aspect of his successful action puzzled many people – how had he been able to sue a French newspaper in an English court when Lord Goodman, acting for Prime Minister Harold Wilson who had a similar problem, had not been able to do so with the Paris-based *International Herald Tribune*?

The answer was that although the *Herald Tribune* published in France on its own presses, it was incorporated in the United States and the writ had to be served there, not in France. Connery's lawyers were able to serve a writ in France because *France-Soir* was a French company.

As Connery observed: 'I think it was Erica Jong who once said that it was one thing to be rich but that if you wanted to stay rich you should get yourself a good lawyer. I think she's right.'

There were times when he thought that if he had been really smart he would have hired a publicity machine to keep a parallel image going for him during the whole of the Bond period. It might have made things easier for him. 'But then I kept asking myself: is it really worth it just to create another image for myself? After all, they'd just be two sides of a Mickey Mouse coin and neither would be me anyway.'

16

Work That Appeals

The real Sean Connery sat relaxed in his south London home clad in his bathrobe, slippered feet on a coffee table, savouring the events of 1968. The onset of Christmas was always a time for reflection and he knew one thing for certain. This would be the last winter he spent in England. Out in Marbella, where the temperature hovered in the high seventies and grapefruit and lemons grew on the trees in his garden, was where he decided he would spend every Christmas in future.

Not this one, of course. He had just come back from a short break in Marbella and this year he was going to spend Christmas in Australia with the family where they would stay with Diane Cilento's parents. Young Jason, who was now five, bounded in, interrupting his thoughts. 'Get back upstairs you dirty rat,' he said affectionately.

He had decided to live a little. He had money in the bank, golf clubs in the cupboard and a pile of scripts to read in his study, but he still felt this curious Celtic guilt complex about his wealth. 'When I was young,' he said at this time, 'even when I had no money, I used to go to Harrods to buy jars of caviar. I couldn't afford it, but I loved the stuff and the guilt I felt about going up to the counter and asking for it was — well, terrible.

Now he had a sauna in the basement of his London home and next to it he had installed an expensive shower which shot hot and cold water at you at the same time. 'It cost me £290 and I thought: what am I doing? What's wrong with the shower in the bathroom upstairs? No, with my background you never lose your guilt complex about money. Not when it comes to spending it. I have no guilt whatsoever about earning it.'

And he felt he had earned it mostly the hard way in the past twelve

months. There had been *The Molly Maguires*, the £3·5 million
Martin Ritt production in Pennsylvania with that hell-raiser,
Richard Harris. A tough one, that. He still carried some of the
bruises as a legacy.

They had staged a reproduction of what was supposed to be a
friendly game, an 1876 football match which was a sort of
roughshod cross between soccer and rugby. He had led one team
and Harris the other, having refused to allow doubles to take their
places. Connery wished he had allowed the doubles. Players had
been left strewn across the pitch as though it had been a battlefield.
Well, it had been a battle. Harris had come away with a black eye, a
broken nose and sore ribs, and as for Connery himself, he had
twisted his right knee and badly bruised his shoulder. Even the Irish
referee Malachy McCourt, who ran a bar in New York called
'Himself', had been kicked in the beard in the process, thereby
impairing his judgment of the game.

When Connery had tried to play golf on the course at Hazleton
nearby he found that water which had swelled into his knee affected
his swing, and that hurt him even more.

He had been left slightly stirred but unshaken by the somewhat
tepid reception given by the critics to *Shalako*, which had been
released in Britain in December, following a world premiere in
Munich in September. Some had admiration for the way in which he
had shaken off the Bond image, but the general feeling seemed to be
that here was another cardboard character. 'For this film a
cardboard character is all you want,' he told them at the usual
reception which accompanied these affairs. 'They were going to try
and give him a lot of depth and background but in a Western like
this we decided to keep him a mystery figure. The public seem to like
an image. I've broken away from the Bond one and given them
another, I hope.'

Brigitte Bardot, who had been wont to travel the dusty roads to
the film's location in Almeria in her all-white Rolls-Royce, as
befitted a sex symbol married to a millionaire, flew in to be with him
for the premiere in London amid reports that she had lost her Sachs
appeal and was separating from Gunther. They were presented to
Princess Margaret, smiling together.

Connery, in fact, had found her rather cool during the making of
the film. 'She's all girl,' he admitted, 'but if I must say so, all on the
outside.'

He had gone to Brussels to help promote the film, where he took champagne with Princess Paola of Belgium and fitted in a round of golf with ex-King Leopold who made up a foursome with two leading Belgian players. He was now playing, with the aid of aluminium-shafted Wilson woods, Ben Sayers irons and a ping-putter that was four inches longer than is usual, off a handicap of 9 with the Stage Golfing Society at Richmond, and a handicap of 12 at Sunningdale.

With his new-found power and ability to command money, Connery was planning to sponsor a charity golf tournament in which Bing Crosby, Bob Hope and Andy Williams would take part as a curtain-raiser to the Open Golf championship at St Andrews the following year. They would play over the old course at Troon in Ayrshire and he flew there to discuss details with the club committee. However, he was also going to listen to Bing Crosby first because he wanted to model the organization of his own invitation as closely as possible on the American star's system. He was going to play in the Bing Crosby tournament in California and would talk to him there. 'Bing has had twenty years to perfect things and find out all the pitfalls,' he said.

Another part of the Connery plan was to set aside some of the profits from his tournament to help subsidize a political survey into the reason why Scots left Scotland. And it would be carried out by St Andrews University, which had turned him down as rector.

In December 1968 the Scottish Nationalists decided to ask him to stand as their prospective Member of Parliament for West Fife. Everyone was enthusiastic until it was discovered that he was not a card-carrying member of the party and therefore not eligible to be chosen as a candidate. 'It's a pity, really,' said a downcast constituency secretary. 'We think he could have won us a lot of votes. Particularly from women.'

Would Sean Connery, who disliked politicians and had never cast a vote in a ballot box in his entire life, have stood as a Member of Parliament? There is no doubt that he took the idea seriously at first, so strongly did he feel about the mismanagement of Scottish affairs. But when he had had time to think it over he said: 'I would not be so presumptuous to sit for any political candidacy without sufficient work, the background and the knowledge. I suppose it would be easy enough to get lieutenants to spoon-feed me, but I'm not familiar enough with all the details across the country. And it's not my style to be spoon-fed. Besides, I'd get found out.'

The year 1969 seemed to speed by for this man of independent views and even more independent financial means. The money positively rolled in: $1 million for *The Molly Maguires* (which was pretty hefty compensation for water on the knee), plus percentage payments from the Bond films which were being re-issued as double bills. 'I'm told the producers were offered $20 million by C.B.S. of America for the whole series for television,' he said. 'And they turned it down. That gives you some idea of what the re-issues must be worth. I've got percentages of the last four, so it pleases me to see them doing well.'

At this time, life appeared to be one perpetual round of golf interspersed with the odd distractions of work that appealed to him; he strictly limited the calls on his time and patience. Often he was unavailable altogether.

'I won't take any messages when I'm out on the course,' he explained. 'I find that if I'm playing golf I can't really think about anything else. It's hard to explain the fascination of the game to anyone who isn't a golfer himself. To me it's a complete revelation of all my shortcomings and problems – temper, ego, feeling, thinking. That's why it's so therapeutic. It almost gives you a philosophy, which is a great help to somebody like myself who doesn't have a religion.'

He was laying out all the money for his tournament initially because he could easily afford it, but he was also out looking for banks, whisky distilleries, newspapers and similar organizations to sponsor each hole. They also could afford it, he reasoned.

And they did. With £15,000 prize money, the Connery tournament was going to be the richest pro-am event ever staged in Britain at that time and with thousands of spectators expected (they reckoned they would have to limit attendances to 15,000 a day), all eighteen holes were rapidly snapped up by eager commercial sponsors at £1,000 a hole.

In April 1969 he visited Russia for the first time to work on the film *The Red Tent*, a first-ever joint Russian-Italian production in which he was playing the part of Roald Amundsen, the Norwegian explorer, for which he had to have his hair dyed a silvery blond.

He entered the Soviet Union, where films like *From Russia With*

Love were banned, wearing a countryman's peaked cap and a rather rustic ensemble of jerkin, open-necked shirt and corduroys. He enjoyed being able to walk around Moscow 'with nobody knowing me from a currant bun', as he put it. But he found the lack of attention frustrating after a while, particularly when he had to break down his own dressing room door when the girl who had the key could not be found. The *coup de grâce* was delivered when he was invited to the British Embassy Club for a fortifying pint of bitter, and a Foreign Office policeman turned him away at the door. The policeman said he did not recognize him and Connery later told his film colleagues that it was his 'worst entrance and best exit' for a long time.

One thing he noted. 'For all their Nijinskys they can't dance. I went to a restaurant in Leningrad and there was a great balalaika band, but the Russians dancing to it were hopeless. All out of step. They wouldn't have lasted ten minutes at the Dennistoun Palais back home.'

Peter Finch had spent nine months of his life on the film, playing the main character Nobile, the Italian Arctic explorer of the twenties, but such was Connery's drawing power that after three weeks' work he was the one to receive star billing.

In November he turned to stage direction again, directing his wife Diane Cilento in a play called *I've Seen You Cut Lemons*. It was written by Ted Allan Herman, the Canadian who had also been responsible for *The Secret of the World* which had been staged in New York, and it left a bitter taste in critics' mouths.

Diane Cilento, partnered by Robert Hardy, played the part of a mentally disturbed sister with a guilty affection for her brother. This enabled her to blow her top, wallow in self-pity, be shrewish, spiteful and tender. She also had to strip down to her underwear and reveal one or two more obvious reasons why her intellectual brother became sexually disturbed at the sight of her.

The suggestion of incest hardly made the critics' hearts grow fonder when it opened at the Fortune Theatre in December. They called the play 'an emotional dustbin'. And what aggrieved Connery was the suggestion that it was a self-indulgent choice both for the director and the players. He shrugged it off by saying: 'If I were one of the actors, considering the work they do and are doing, I would be upset and annoyed. But being in the chair as director one has to be much more philosophical.'

In between these bouts of work and golf, he had also been writing a screenplay for a film of Macbeth which he thought could be revolutionary. 'I believe the violence and sex in the eleventh and twelfth centuries is all there in Scotland today.'

Scotland and its problems continued to occupy him until well into the New Year, and in February 1970 he sat with a dutiful Diane Cilento by his side in the stands at Parkhead, Glasgow, looking every inch the contented soccer fan in cloth cap and tweed jacket, pulling on a pipe as he watched Celtic beat Rangers 3–1 in the Scottish Cup.

Less than a month later he and actor Stanley Baker went to play in the Moroccan golf championships in Marrakesh and Mohammedia near Casablanca. And it was there, on the golf course, that he met an attractive Frenchwoman. Born in Nice and brought up mainly in South Africa, she was a divorcee with a son, and had been a Mrs Cosman. She could cook well and she could play golf off a 17 handicap.

She introduced herself as Micheline. Micheline Roquebrune.

17

Back in Bondage

Sean Connery was now a grizzled forty-year-old and a millionaire. By mid-1970 the Bond film *Goldfinger* alone had made £20 million around the world, according to Harry Saltzman. And the question that was beginning to plague him and his cohorts as they sampled the delights of Las Vegas was how they could tempt this millionaire film star and sportsman turned businessman back into Bondage.

Outside of the Royal Mint, a Bond film plus Connery had been the best way of lawfully coining money they had ever known, and after the traumas they had gone through with George Lazenby playing Bond in their latest 007 epic *On Her Majesty's Secret Service*, they needed him. Everyone thought that picture could have been the best of the bunch if Connery had continued in the role. Instead, they had been lumbered with Lazenby who had turned out to have a head as big as the giant chocolate bar he had humped across the television screen in the Big Fry commercial.

After Lazenby, a Bond team consisting of Cubby Broccoli, Guy Hamilton and the designer Ken Adam had gone to the United States in the hope of finding an American actor to play the part. They worked at Universal studios and tested a number of them, including John Gavin, a great friend of Ronnie Reagan who was later to become U.S. ambassador to Mexico.

The film was to be *Diamonds Are Forever* and they already had several girls lined up, including Jill St John, once married to the Woolworth heir Lance Reventlow, who told everyone that her longest period of celibacy was the shortest distance between two lovers and Lana Wood, sister of Natalie Wood, who had made her debut baring all in an issue of *Playboy* magazine which had led everyone to cry: 'Oh my gaaaahd! We gotta have that chick!' and promptly cast her as Miss Plenty O'Toole.

The problem was that with Connery out of the running there were very few actors around capable of handling the sardonic humour and the throwaway lines, or of getting to the high pleasure points of an audience with such devastating effect as Connery. 'With Connery, Jill St John would be perfect,' said Guy Hamilton, 'but, hell, we haven't *got* Connery.'

They had lost all direct communication with the man since he had quit at the end of *You Only Live Twice*, vowing that he would never return. Saltzman said, quite accurately, 'He wouldn't even speak to either of us now.' Cubby Broccoli, reluctant to leave the craps table while the dice were still rolling on the Bond films, suggested a new approach. 'He'd talk to Sopel,' he said.

Stanley Sopel, associate producer, immediately arranged an appointment with Richard Hatton, Connery's agent, for the following week. In London at the Dorchester Hotel in December 1970 the three men met, covering a great deal of ground while consuming a bottle of Scotch in the process. 'I finally mentioned a magnificent figure,' says Sopel, 'and Sean just laughed. He didn't budge. I couldn't do a deal with him but to give you an idea of how good a businessman he was becoming, he did a deal with me. He sold me a Mercedes from a second-hand car business he had acquired in East London.'

When Sopel reported back to Broccoli and Saltzman they told him to forget it. 'But I had the feeling that Sean was very interested,' Sopel said. 'I'm sure he doesn't need the money, but I think he realizes his career needs a little uplift.' With time running short and pressure to start the picture now coming from New York, where United Artists needed a vintage Bond quickly, Broccoli in desperation signed John Gavin for the role. The president of United Artists, David Picker, had already fixed the opening dates, before the production had a star or even a script.

Picker decided to nail Connery himself. At the end of February 1971, as the production date loomed in Las Vegas, he flew to London and made Connery a final offer that proved irresistible.

The deal was done at the Dorchester and took days of negotiation. It finally included a promise by United Artists to back two further pictures of Connery's choice which would have nothing to do with Bond, $1,250,000 in cash (at that time around £520,000) to be paid over the eighteen weeks he would work on the Bond production, and a percentage of the profits. He was on 10 per cent of the gross. 'And my instructions,' says Sopel, 'were to pay the first million-dollar cheque in advance directly into the Scottish bank of which Connery was a director. How about that?'

To appreciate Connery's own business acumen in clinching the deal it is necessary to trace events immediately preceding it. During 1970 he had been involved in the formation of the Scottish International Education Trust which was launched in early December 1970 with Sir Iain Stewart of Fairfields fame as the chairman and himself as vice chairman. It was Connery's version of the American Dream, an ambitious project to sell Scotland to Scots abroad and thus help reverse the emigration trend. 'Make no mistake about it,' he said at the launching in Edinburgh, 'Scots abroad owe their country something and I'm after at least £1 a head from émigrés. There's obviously something wrong if Scots keep abandoning their country. What we are trying to do is improve the country so that people will not be so ready to move.'

The Connery-Stewart merger was based on the friendship of the fairways and the locker-and-boardroom brotherhood. They did business together, played golf together and dined together often in the grill room of the Dorchester, which was another of Stewart's directorships, and they flew to their villas in Spain together. They exchanged jokes with a Scots accent and dialect no Englishman could understand without an interpreter, and business rivals were made aware that at a conference table they could also exchange vital messages in the Scots idiom.

Together they had also developed some non-charitable, less altruistic interests. One of them was a private bank with panelled offices in Pall Mall which rejoiced in the very Scottish name of Dunbar and Co. Sean Connery was one of six directors of the bank, which opened with capital of £250,000 and offered all banking services. They had acquired a wide range of customers, including a number from the world of showbusiness.

It was into this bank that £17,000 of the money raised by Sean Connery's pro-am tournament at Troon earlier that year was deposited for the Educational Trust, and into which further funds would go as he set up a series of sports spectaculars on its behalf. He had also deposited his own money there, and here, too, went the million or so dollars he was being paid for *Diamonds Are Forever*, which he had decided to give to the Trust as his personal donation to the cause.

'I was only going to do the Bond film because I could give $1 million to the Trust,' he says, 'so I'm not such an idiot as to forget the money and fame Bond brought me. It may look like it at times but I'm not really the kind of man to spend the rest of his life solely on golf courses and in bars. My sort of upbringing gave me an urge to be useful and to contribute what you can. I've been lucky to do a lot of the taking.'

However, as he admitted drily one afternoon when talking about his private bank: 'One of the troubles with having a lot of money is that you have to keep watching those who are paid to watch it. Being a director of a bank I can watch it myself. Which I do. Everything I have is deposited there. I think a private bank is good for people in our profession and I'll tell you why. People in a public bank can see how much you earn and if you are split with your wife what payments you make – and that's how rumours start.'

He had a very special reason for keeping his affairs safe from prying eyes at this time. He had a talent for secrecy, an inbuilt Celtic trait for being devious. It was a form of self-protection. It happened with money. And it happened with love. His marriage to Diane Cilento was, to all intents and purposes, over. They had always had the problems of conflicting careers, which they had tried to solve, but the questions they kept asking themselves over the years always kept cropping up with deadening monotony whenever a part was offered: *What's she doing? What's he doing? Who'll look after the kids? Can they come? Who'll take care of the house?* Interminable. A travelling circus was not the answer for a loner such as he was. Moving around with managers and housekeepers and secretaries was not his way of life at all. With Diane over the past few years it had been like putting two pint pots into one. It had not worked and now they were spilling over.

As he says: 'One is always reluctant to admit failure, and a marriage that goes wrong is as bad as anything can be. We had to step back and see what we were doing to one another. To our lives and to the lives of our son and daughter. We were not incompatible as people but our careers were. So we finally had to come to terms that what we'd got ourselves into. The children, fortunately, knew the situation and were great.'

But that was only part of it. In the months since he had met Micheline Roquebrune in Morocco the marriage had been under particular strain and he was not a man to confide in anyone. 'I've never had a true confidante in my life, not even when I was married to Diane. To be honest, I can never remember having a great dissertation with anybody. I just make up my own mind and get on with it. Anyway, I'm much too suspicious to take anybody's advice about anything.'

They had separated once before and since then Diane Cilento had tried hard to carve out a career of her own that would dovetail with his lifestyle. She had written a second novel (it was called *Hybrid*) so that she could spend more time at home as a wife and mother, but now that he was mulling over the prospect of playing Bond yet again, a role which she had always felt made her nothing more than a cipher, the time had come for a parting of the ways. 'In the end,' she says, 'I walked out on him.'

Their separation came in February 1971 when he returned from a golfing holiday in Spain. 'This time it *is* the end,' he acknowledged. He remained at their Putney home and she went to live in Wimbledon near the All-England Tennis Club. That way, living within a five-minute drive of one another, they could both see the children. However, she was also intent on picking up the threads of her own film career again and planned to make a picture in Denmark with Oliver Reed called *The First of January*. It seemed like a good omen to start a new life.

The following month Sean Connery flew off to Tunisia for three golf tournaments with Graham Hill the racing driver, Ronnie Carroll, Stanley Baker and Eric Sykes. And later that month he was proposed for membership of the venerable home of golf, the 217-year-old Royal and Ancient at St Andrews. He was sponsored by Sir Iain Stewart and it was a singular honour because this was the cradle of the game and to be a member was the ultimate status symbol for any golfer.

Life was good except for when he returned to his Putney home. He surveyed the emptiness and became aware, almost for the first time, of the importance of a woman in the place. 'She's the real governing factor, not the man,' he observed. 'Someone like my grandfather could come home and kick everybody in sight and chuck his food in the fireplace and it didn't make the slightest difference. Life went on. The children grew up. Whatever the man does, the real influence in the home is the woman.'

Without a woman the Putney house was no longer a home and he decided to put it on the market. At that time it was valued at around

£35,000 and he felt the need to be rid of it quickly. After all, he reasoned, he too had to make a new life for himself.

18

The Vegas Gamble

Out on the Las Vegas Strip, the men who were the biggest gamblers in showbusiness were embarked on the greatest gamble of their Midas-rich lives. They were staking $7 million, or something a little under £3 million, as their bet that James Bond in the shape of a forty-year-old Sean Connery was not a has-been. As soon as the former 007 flew into this plastic oasis in the Nevada desert a newspaper had put a question to all its readers: 'Don't you think 007 with his double chin and middle-aged hairline looks a fright?'

To Cubby Broccoli lying naked on the health club massage table above the Riviera casino, and to Harry Saltzman playing the fruit machines with nickels from a paper cup, risk was indispensable to fortune. And the risk, after six smash hits inside ten years, was that the public would not buy another Bond fantasy, particularly with a hero who was even then arguing with his hairdresser about the hairpieces that had been flown in from London. 'He would prefer to play Bond as a balding hero,' his hairdresser said. 'He keeps telling me to thin out his wigs until there is almost no point in him wearing them at all.'

Connery said: 'Age is as inevitable as tomorrow. Nobody is immortal, not me, not you, and not James Bond. This fascination for looking young is the joke of all time.' In a town obsessed with cosmetic aids to beauty and youth and where they had, mercifully, made it illegal for losers at the tables to pawn artificial limbs, hearing aids or false teeth, he sometimes felt that he must be the only real and honest human being around.

Perhaps it is why, when he wasn't filming, the kind of company Connery chose to keep was that of men like comedians Alan King and Buddy Hackett, a former New Jersey cop who wore a Derringer pistol strapped to his right calf and had a sign put up at his home which read: 'If you're found on these premises at night, you'll be found here in the morning.'

Such men amused Connery because, as he said: 'They are so bloody competitive and I find that quality in a man very attractive. It doesn't have to be a race, or a game of golf or a woman, but just scoring off life itself.' Not for nothing was there a smile on his face as he and the glamorous Jill St John, that great and good friend of then American Secretary of State Henry Kissinger, made love in *Diamonds Are Forever* on a luxurious waterbed holding 700 gallons of salt water and 3,000 tropical fish frantically darting to and fro beneath their amorous couplings.

Connery had never lost his own acquisitiveness and probably never would, however rich he became. 'I can still remember the first time I flew,' he said. 'I swiped everything that wasn't nailed down to the fuselage – the maps, safety instructions, cologne from the toilets, even those little tubes of mustard.'

And what his friends liked about Connery was his complete honesty and lack of conceit. As Alan King described it: 'He never once acted like he owned the joint. That's pretty rare for a guy in his position. But then you also figure he knows something that you don't know. It makes you treat him with a little more respect.'

Sean Connery did know something that they did not know. He moved among waiters, cab drivers and barmen with a style which earned him the respectful familiarity they might show to a class fighter or a top gangster because he knew the score. As Guy Hamilton said: 'You don't bullshit Connery.'

On this new Bond film Connery had a start-stop clause in his contract stipulating the date on which his services would be withdrawn. Should the production run into difficulties and be prolonged beyond that date, he would be compensated for the extra time he might be required to work at the rate of $145,000 a week.

He revelled in this kind of deal. 'It can be done if there's money at stake,' he says. 'I'd been frigged about too much on other Bond pictures as a result of bad decisions being made at the top.'

Movie tycoonery fascinated Connery. Moguls like Darryl F. Zanuck, Louis B. Mayer and Jack L. Warner were of consuming interest because they had become remote from reality and their decisions could never be genuinely questioned other than by men who were tougher than they were. 'Remember that film producer in the book *The Godfather* who had the head of his racehorse cut off by the Mafia? That incident is supposed to be true and the producer is alleged to be modelled on Jack Warner.' In the light of such stories, apocryphal or not, he confessed there was a certain piquancy to his recollection of how he had 'screwed Jack Warner for $50,000' when the film *A Fine Madness* had overrun its shooting schedule.

Guy Hamilton brought *Diamonds Are Forever* in on time in the eighteen weeks scheduled for shooting in four different countries and dozens of locations. In Connery's view the production team had made a highly professional job of what was a highly complex operation.

He admired efficiency. 'It's like watching a good racehorse, or the way Picasso works where everything functions within its capacity. But talking to some top moguls about my idea of efficiency is like trying to describe to someone who has never taken exercise what it is like when you *do* take exercise. They don't understand.'

Stanley Sopel says that in those first ten years of collaboration Broccoli and Saltzman made a perfect team. 'Cubby was the practical man. Problems in shooting, or personal relationships – he would sort those out. Harry was the one with the great ideas. At a production meeting he would come up with about twenty of them which were either impractical or too costly, but every so often he would come up with a gem.'

Connery put Harry's success rate at about one good idea in eight and his opinion of the Broccoli-Saltzman partnership at this time was that he did not think they were exactly enamoured of one another. 'Probably because they are both sitting on £50 million and looking across the desk at each other and thinking: "That bugger's got half of what should be all mine," ' he said.

The team's gamble, the $7 million question, 'Can James Bond still be the world's most popular wish fulfilment at forty?' was answered at the box office in due course.

The previous six Bond films had by now made a total of £80 million. A year later, *Variety*, the showbusiness newspaper known throughout the industry as 'The Bible', calculated that by the time *Diamonds Are Forever* had finished playing around the world, Sean Connery could expect to make $6 million.

When the man who had always seemed enmeshed in the myth of the character James Bond arrived back in England for the finish of that picture he felt that he had accomplished quite a few things and

Bathtime during *You Only Live Twice*, 1966

Sucking a sea-urchin sting from Claudine Auger's foot in *Thunderball*, 1965

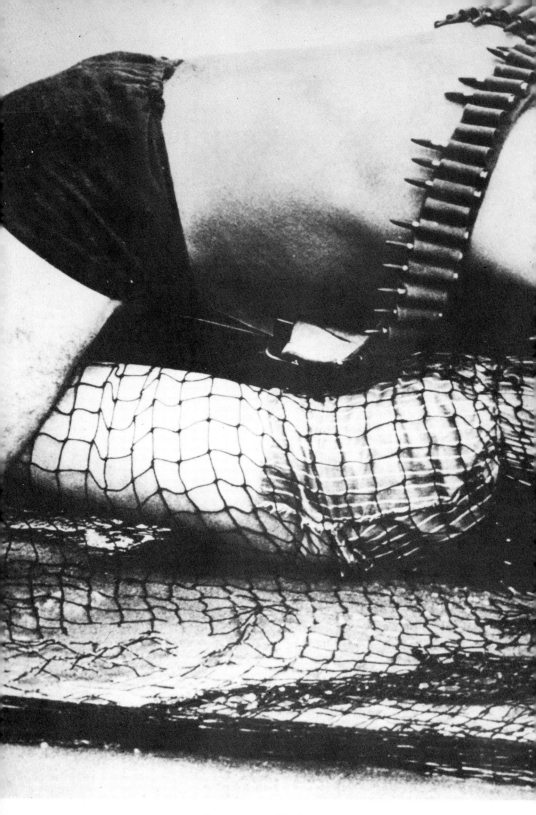

A scene from *Zardoz*, 1974

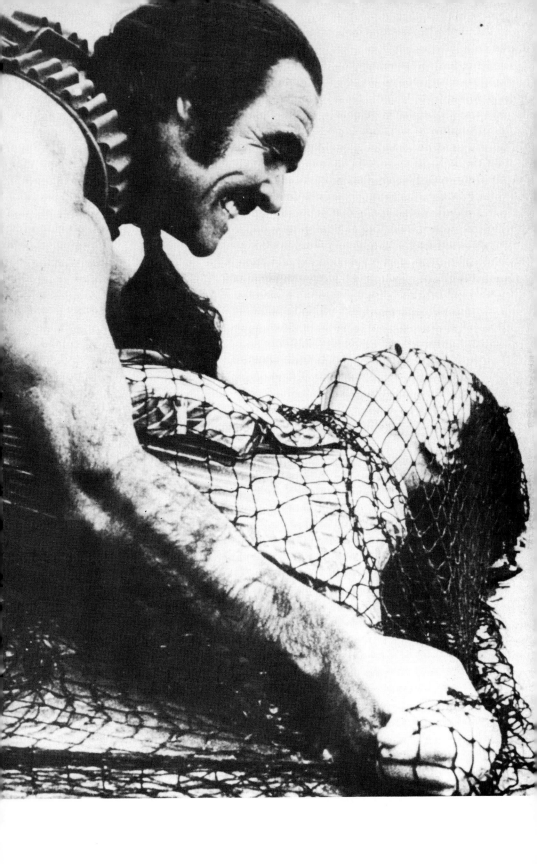

With Brooke Adams during filming of *Cuba*, 1979

With his wife Micheline, March 1981

With son Jason in August 1982

had bought a little breathing space to look at his life, decide what to withdraw from, what to reach for, and what he really needed. One thing he did not need was what he described as 'the maniacal power' that the money coming to him now might generate. He had seen Onassis in Claridges looking as though he enjoyed himself with his airline and his yacht and his private island in the sun, but that was his life and he was not sure what his own should be, but it would not be that.

'The trouble with money is that you cannot have it and just not do something about it,' he said. 'And I do not ever intend to be in the position of having to worry about it. A lot of people may think I'm mad not be living in the Bahamas or whatever, but I have this basic reluctance to be indulgent. It's a Scottish thing. I dislike indulgent people living in the Bahamas moaning about having to live in the Bahamas.'

It had taken him three years to get his Scottish Educational Trust accepted as a charity and once that had been done he had been able to let them have his million dollars of Bond money from the *Diamonds Are Forever* deal tax free. 'It's an opportunity that doesn't come often in a man's life,' he said wryly.

At forty he figured he was more than half-way dead and he decided he would have to spend the next few months putting his life into some sort of order. He needed someone to manage his financial affairs, to put them in perspective. 'It's hopeless having everything in one bag – one's emotional life, one's career and one's financial affairs. That way each of them has equal importance and they're not equally important. And if you have them all lumped together in one bag they're inter-effective, like a rotten apple. Trouble with one means trouble with them all.'

He was still deeply concerned about the breakdown of his marriage, but everything seemed to be sorting itself out in a civilized way at this stage.

Connery's first move was to take an apartment on the Embankment overlooking the Thames at Chelsea. It was in a house once occupied by Ribbentrop, the Nazi ambassador to Britain until the outbreak of the Second World War, and it had a wine cellar. 'It also had paintings,' he said, 'but five minutes after Hitler called Ribbentrop back to Berlin, I'm told the neighbours came in and took all the pictures away. You have to admire that. The pictures were probably stolen, anyway.'

He took a boyish delight in such things. After the October premiere of *The Anderson Tapes*, for example, the proceeds of which went to the Educational Trust to help and educate poor children, he played in a golf match to help swell the funds even more. There were several prizes and a raffle for a golf bag. He won three of the prizes and the raffle as well. 'And you know what?' he said. 'I sold the golf bag later for £15.'

He could not have been more delighted. Like most rich men, these small practical gains amused and satisfied him more than the huge amounts of money he was being paid for his work. He could not be objective about his millions, but the blood and sweat and tears that went into parting with £10 or £100 on a golf course was something to which he could relate.

Nevertheless, he did not hesitate to use his new-found power within the film industry. He did it, much to the chagrin of Columbia's top brass, when he insisted that the world premiere of *The Anderson Tapes*, a film he had made before going back to Bond, should be held in Glasgow and not in London so that his Educational Trust would be richer by one charity performance on its home ground.

He planned to fly a party of his friends to Glasgow for that premiere. They included Stanley Baker, Ronnie Corbett, Bruce Forsyth, Ronnie Carroll, Jimmy Tarbuck, Henry Cooper, Ray Barrett, Kenny Lynch, Glen Mason and Michael Medwin. And before take-off three of them received an anonymous phone call threatening their lives if they travelled on the plane. Stanley Baker was threatened with a bomb and Sean Connery and Ronnie Corbett were warned they would be shot.

Connery said: 'The caller told me that he had learned the money made from the premiere would go to help arm Roman Catholics fighting against the Protestants in Northern Ireland. It sounded ridiculous but none of us can afford to take chances.' The party's British Caledonian flight was delayed for fifty minutes at Gatwick while security checks were made and each one of the passengers was asked before take-off to claim their own baggage.

With a clutch of comic talent aboard, jokes relieved the tension. Connery himself can be a good imitator when he is in a light-hearted, conversational mood and he enjoyed the company of comedians. Not surprisingly, he particularly admired Scottish comics like Jimmy Logan and those who could play around with words surrealistically. One of his favourite examples of north of the Border humour at this time was the Scots comedian Chic Murray whom he would copy in the dialect: 'I was walking out of the house the other day putting my left foot in front of my right foot because that's the usual way I walk. And I saw my auntie and I said: "Hello, dear." I always call her dear because she's got antlers.' The party was in very good form by the time they reached Glasgow.

Directed by Sidney Lumet, *The Anderson Tapes* was a film in which Connery played a murderous ex-convict. Instead of the suave mix of gallantry and invulnerability that had made Connery's Bond a cross between Young Lochinvar and the Marquis de Sade, here the man was mouthing four-letter words, making clumsy love, monumental mistakes and unheroic concessions. The film and Connery's performance were well received by the critics and public alike. In America it was reported to have taken $3 million in the first nine weeks. It boded well for the future now that his love-hate affair with the character of Bond, which had spanned ten years of his life, was over.

19

Independent Film-Maker

It was Christmas Day 1971 but all was far from festive in the Forsyth family household. As Sean Connery lay on a bed watching television with Bruce Forsyth after the traditional turkey and plum pudding, you could have cut the atmosphere with a carving knife. Which was precisely what the comedian's wife, Penny Forsyth, seething in the kitchen downstairs, was about to do.

Sean Connery had spent most of the year adjusting himself to a bachelor lifestyle after he and Diane Cilento had separated. Occasionally he went to dinner with Diane and the children Giovanna, who was then fourteen, and Jason, his nine-year-old son, and the children visited him at his riverside flat when they came home from their private schools. He collected them personally from the station instead of sending a chauffeur because, as he said, 'they are important to me'. So far, everything had seemed to run fairly smoothly and this Christmas the children had been invited to spend the day at the Forsyth home with him. But for his golfing companion Bruce Forsyth things were not running smoothly at all.

After a series of separations from his wife he had come back home for the holiday to be with the family (he had three daughters), and the afternoon lull after lunch was being punctuated by an irritating number of phone calls made by a tearful girl in search of him.

Finally, an irate Penny Forsyth went upstairs to tell him to talk to the girl. According to her account Sean Connery took one look at her and sensing her mood said: 'Here we go.' He was told to stay out of it. Bruce Forsyth picked up the phone and reached for a diary his wife had been given to write down the girl's address. His wife grabbed the diary back and hit him on the head with it, whereupon Sean sighed and, pulling a fiver from his pocket, gave it to Bruce to write down the necessary details. And when Penny Forsyth went downstairs to the kitchen he followed her there. As she picked up the knife she had used to carve the Christmas turkey he took it from her saying: 'You stupid Irish —— what do you think you're doing?'

He knew very well what she was contemplating and he moved swiftly to diffuse the situation. 'He took me into the lounge and began talking to me. He was the most fantastic person and when I asked what Bruce was doing he said: "You know very well what he's doing. He's packing."'

The incident reminded Sean Connery of the time he had been to a party at which the theatre critic Kenneth Tynan had been present when there was a fight between two men over a girl. 'Tynan helped to separate the men,' he says, 'and do you know what he said? He said: "Stop behaving like people." That man must have been waiting all his life for a situation where he could make a remark like that.'

The year had ended with the critics welcoming *Diamonds Are Forever* as a cure for anyone's post-Christmas depression, which reflected how, like good wine, Connery had matured over the years. They singled out for special applause the deceptive ease with which he now handled his more sophisticated epigrams such as the murmured 'You've caught me with more than my hands up' as his love-making was interrupted. He had arrived at the press preview of that picture with Roger Moore, thus giving rise to speculation that the Saint would now be taking over from the Sinner. Asked what the difference would be if he took over the 007 role, Roger Moore simply flashed a grin and said: 'My teeth are whiter.'

In the meantime, Connery, having arranged an Edinburgh premiere of *Diamonds Are Forever* for his Educational Trust, had been spending some of his Bond money. Apart from the million dollars apiece United Artists had agreed to give him to back two pictures of his own choosing, his deal had also included an extra $100,000 dollars as 'exploration money'. This was for developing scripts and he had earlier taken a holiday in Spain for that purpose. Now he had set up an independent film company called Tantallon to make a film version of John Hopkins's powerful stage drama *This Story Is Yours*, which had first been seen at the Royal Court Theatre a couple of seasons before. Connery wanted to star as the police interrogator and with his own money and his own company he could do just as he pleased.

It seemed as though he could control most things these days, other than the inevitable passage of time. He was forty-one when his father died in March 1972 and it had a profound effect upon him. 'He was sixty-nine, my father, and somehow I had never thought of him dying. He was such a contented man. And when he did die it was a great stopper for me. It brought me up with a tremendous jolt. The doctor had shown me his X-rays and discussed cobalt treatment and then said there was no hope. Only a year before the X-rays had been clear. I had retired him when he was about sixty and he was loving every minute of it. Now he's dead and it's a sobering experience, more than I ever realized it would be. You know, there's a saying in the Masai tribe that you are not a man until your father dies. If that is true, then it is a pretty stiff price to pay.'

His father's death brought about a period of self-examination in Sean Connery. He had stopped smoking cigarettes some years earlier, cutting the habit completely. He had tried smoking pot and although he admitted the weed turned him on he had not continued with it because it was too much like smoking cigarettes. He had taken to cigars instead and he smoked them with the band on, something that James Bond would never have done. But by this time Connery had experienced more than the fictional Bond ever would, which made him much more his own man than Bond would ever be. A vulnerable man still, but much, much tougher.

He drank large Scotch whiskies, preferring his native brew to vodka, the sales of which he had sent rocketing during the Bond years but which was not his tipple at all, and he was trying hard to pace himself now because when he drank he drank too much and too easily and suffered hangovers as a result. He had also learned that he dehydrated very quickly, especially in high temperatures. When he had been making *You Only Live Twice* in Japan they had had to pump a pint of saline into him when he was slowing down without realizing it, and on *The Molly Maguires* the doctors had given him tea with a whole lemon squeezed into it and some salt crackers. Both remedies had worked.

Inevitably over the years he had acquired a taste for the sybaritic but it still bothered him. It was why he could visit an up-market strip club such as Raymond's Revuebar in London's Soho to admire female flesh presented with style and at the same time wince at the price of champagne. And it was why he could sit in fashionable showbusiness haunts surveying the expense-account eaters with a proletarian disdain, saying: 'That's the trouble with the film industry. All these marvellous plans for reforming it, but catch any of these producers foregoing posh suits and extravagant lunches. That's where the money goes.'

Asked whether there were any women in his life at this period he smiled and said: 'Well, there's my Portuguese housekeeper, my secretary and my fourteen-year-old daughter Giovanna.' However, in early April, when he was working on his new film which had the provisional title *Something Like The Truth*, there at his side at Twickenham studios was the auburn-haired Frenchwoman he had met in Morocco, Micheline Roquebrune. And during the year she became firmly ensconced in his Embankment flat. It was a magnificent four-bedroomed apartment with three bathrooms, three reception rooms, high moulded ceilings, panelled walls, oak beams and views across the Thames.

His views on women he made known to Roderick Mann, the showbusiness columnist of the *Sunday Express*. He said: 'I don't seem to have the equipment for marriage in terms of the contract as it exists today. But I would like more children and, of course, I would want them to be by a woman who would bring them up properly. But who knows what will happen? The only difference in my attitude to women today is that I now make my position quite clear from the start. In the past I used to get involved and just let events take their course. I used to fall into the trap of believing that because you thought something regarding a woman it was just like saying it. But it isn't, is it? Where women are concerned you have got to say it.'

Whether this was a guide to Micheline no one knew because he did not even mention her.

For his first project as an independent film-maker Sean Connery had invested in some considerable talent. As a director he had Sidney Lumet with whom he had made *The Hill* and *The Anderson Tapes*, which was now an international screen success. In his cast he had Trevor Howard, Vivien Merchant and Ian Bannen, with himself playing the leading role as a detective named Johnson. It was a difficult part, that of a failed policeman who interrogates a man suspected of molesting a child, a man who dies under his relentless questioning. When he, in turn, is then interrogated, he has to do the talking and reveal himself, a painful exercise in character analysis.

He wondered how the public would take it after his Bond success. *Diamonds Are Forever* had now broken every cinema attendance record everywhere it played, from Japan to Chicago, from Sweden to St Louis. It was a licence to print money, even then racing away to a total gross of $100 million.

His own film was a new challenge and he worked hard at the role, at times up to twenty hours a day, and the professionalism was evident when he brought in the film, now titled *The Offence*, £25,000 below its £400,000 budget. He said he had never felt so happy or fulfilled about anything he had done in his career so far. But artistic satisfaction was one thing. Audience reaction was another. That could only be gauged at the box office where his company had a 50 per cent share of the returns.

The rest of the year he spent sorting out his varied business interests, discarding those that no longer interested him, among them a country club project in which he had invested together with Bobby Moore, the England soccer star. He was not an idle man and attending to the affairs of his Educational Trust, looking for scripts, and playing golf at the standard he did now, kept him fully occupied. He had been admitted to the prized membership of the Royal and Ancient Golf Club and in September he and his partner Sir Iain Stewart powered their way to the final of the Calcutta Cup at St Andrews only to be beaten 2 and 1 by their opponents. October found him in the Mediterranean resort of La Manga in Spain for a pro-am golf tournament where, despite his denials, close friends were predicting among themselves that he and Micheline Roquebrune would eventually marry, so close had their relationship become.

By the year's end he was voted Britain's favourite actor at the box office and *Diamonds Are Forever* the year's biggest money-spinner. He went off on holiday to Spain that Christmas with Micheline and when they returned after New Year celebrations in early January 1973 they were confronted with the critics' verdict on *The Offence*. Connery found them somewhat dismissive. The general opinion seemed to be that although it was a good example of how to make a British film quickly and efficiently, Sidney Lumet's handling of the story was too aggressive and his own performance over-powerful.

Undeterred, Sean Connery set off for Hamburg on the first leg of a European tour to promote the film, becoming the first star to go into action as a salesman in the Common Market.

He kept on the move. In early March he flew to Nairobi to take part in the Kenya Open Golf Championship. It was becoming clear to his associates that he was preparing the groundwork for a new phase in his eventful life. He put his £95,000 Embankment flat on the market and in May 1973, finding the right scripts difficult to come by for his next project as a producer, he made a snap decision to take over from Burt Reynolds as the star of a film called *Zardoz*. Reynolds had been ordered to take three months' rest and he replaced him in this futuristic thriller with Charlotte Rampling. At the same time he broke a fifteen-year association with his agent Richard Hatton and moved to the prestigious Creative Management Associates agency to be represented by Denis Selinger. And while these negotiations were underway he was having a new and luxurious beach villa built for him in the fashionable resort of Marbella. Supervising the arrangements was Micheline Roquebrune.

In June 1973 Sean Connery decided to go ahead with divorce proceedings against Diane Cilento. His petition appeared that September in the list of undefended cases in the London Divorce Court.

Although they had lived apart for two years, Diane Cilento made no secret of the fact that she wanted to remain married. 'There is no need for a divorce,' she said. According to her friends she had resisted a divorce because she had not given up hope that one day they would get together again as a family, but Connery, after months of legal negotiation, had made up his mind.

In October 1973, at the age of forty-three, he was granted a decree nisi on the grounds that their eleven-year marriage had broken down irretrievably and that they had been parted for the statutory two years.

His counsel, Mr Jeremy Tatham, told the judge: 'The husband and wife not only wish for a civilized end to the marriage by a "two-year divorce", but they wish to end the financial litigation between them for ever. After fifteen months' negotiation I think we have achieved that by capital sums which they would prefer you not to mention in open court. The first is a sum payable to Miss Cilento in full and final settlement of all her claims. The second is a sum setting up a trust for the two children of the family.'

Diane Cilento did not attend the hearing but by agreement she was given the custody of their two children with reasonable access for Sean Connery.

Outside the court, when asked whether he had any plans to re-marry, he made his position crystal clear. 'As from this day,' he said, 'I have no comment to make on my private life. Nothing of my private life will ever be divulged to the press. I do not have a particularly good relationship with the press, partly because I have no press agent. To simplify matters I am keeping my private life private.'

To intimates, however, he said he had no particular desire to marry again. 'I'm not in the market for it at the moment. All Diane and I are concerned about now is making sure the future works for the children.' At the same time, for those who wondered about his constant live-in companion, he admitted: 'Permissive society or not, it's a rare bird indeed who will stay with you year in and year out if you don't marry her.'

20
A Nightmare of Litigation

According to Micheline Roquebrune she and Sean Connery had considered themselves 'married' from the time they began living together. 'As you know, Sean and I first met playing golf at Casablanca. There was this handsome man who came up to me on the course and we started talking. We played golf together, went out several times – and fell in love. It was then that Sean said: "Look here, there's something you've got to know. I play golf three days a week or more. If I can't play that often I get angry and ill-tempered." I burst out laughing and said: "Listen, Sean, I'm not going to be a golf widow. I play golf a lot, too. And if you were not a golfer you would be a golf widower because I won't give it up, even for you." We have lived a great part of our lives on golf courses ever since.'

She was talking in the spring of 1975 in Morocco, where Sean Connery was on location for the film *The Man Who Would Be King*, and she was by his side. A month earlier, at the beginning of March, he had told everyone that he had married her in a secret ceremony, but he refused to say when or where the marriage had taken place. Such was his obsession with privacy. It was suggested by a close friend that they had been married four months earlier in Casablanca and he did not bother to deny it. All he said was: 'When Diane and I separated I vowed I would never again speak about marriage or marrying. I said I would never discuss my private life. But I will tell you now that I am married again.'

As an attempt at subterfuge, a ruse to avoid publicity and persistent questions, it was doomed. Connery was too big a personality for something like a secret marriage to have taken place without anyone knowing. He was, in fact, married two months later, on 6 May 1975, on the Rock of Gibraltar where years before he had gone through a similar simple ceremony with Diane Cilento.

Believing he had put everyone off the scent he was furious when he saw a photographer waiting to take a picture of what he hoped would be a happy, smiling couple. 'If you take my picture, I'll knock your head off,' Connery snarled. And he meant it. After the ceremony the newlyweds flew back to their new home near Marbella where he was now a tax exile.

A few months previously, faced with punitive tax demands if he remained a U.K. subject, he had decided to base himself in Spain and work from there, where many of the films he was offered could be made. However, many of his friends believe that Sean Connery would not have left Britain had the Scottish Nationalists been able to form their own Parliament in October 1974 and create a tax haven of their own. His interest in and commitment to Scotland were well established. As he himself said before the election results were made known: 'The Scots have what is necessary to create a similar situation to the one that exists in Switzerland. They are bankers and they are honest, dependable and trustworthy.'

When it became clear there would be no Scottish tax haven he had been left with the choice of giving the taxman 83p out of every £1 he earned if he stayed in Britain, or of moving out and being allowed back in the country for ninety days a year. For him the choice was obvious. He moved to Spain.

His fellow Celt and close companion Stanley Baker, the Welsh actor later to be recommended for a knighthood by Prime Minister Harold Wilson for his services to the Socialist cause, was reported to have had such a blazing row over Connery's decision to become a tax exile that it had cast a shadow over their friendship, which went back more than twenty years to the days when the Scot often did not have the price of his bus fare back home and would stay with the Bakers for the night. Later in the year, however, they became reconciled.

For Connery 1974 had been a decisive year. In a few months he had acquired a new agent, a new lawyer, a new tax accountant, a divorce, the prospect of a new wife and a new outlook. It had been easy with the kind of money available to him to start a business empire, but it had created a chain reaction with secretaries, minutes, meetings, records, correspondence – a deluge of paper work demanding his time. He had found himself a mogul without the structure to support his empire. As a loner he had to make every decision and in the end it had all become too much. He had dropped everything except the Trust and his film interests. The artistic producing he had wanted to do did not work out the way he had hoped, so he had gone back to what he knew best of all, which was acting.

In January 1974 he had gone to Norway to make the film *Ransom*, a thriller based on the contemporary problem of hijacking, directed by Casper Wrede. He had followed that with his fourth film with Sidney Lumet, *Murder on the Orient Express*, playing Arbuthnot, an Indian Army colonel. With all the talent gathered together for that one – Lauren Bacall, Ingrid Bergman, Albert Finney, Tony Perkins, Vanessa Redgrave and Sir John Gielgud to name but a few – he had felt it had been rather like going back to Bond.

In August he had celebrated his forty-fourth birthday. Cherishing thoughts of home he had invited old friends and golf partners, among them Bruce Forsyth, Stanley Baker, Jimmy Tarbuck and Sir Iain Stewart, to his home near Marbella for a personal golf tournament he had organized at the Atalaya Park Golf Club where he presented prizes for the competition between himself and his guests. Jimmy Tarbuck's present to him had been an instruction book on golf, which had been good for a laugh.

There had been another good reason, too, for remembering his birthday. At the Mau Mau, a beach club frequented by the jet-set fraternity, he had stepped in to prevent a punch-up between the Austrian film star Helmut Berger and a Spanish photographer who had tried to snatch pictures of Berger dancing with Tina Onassis, the Greek ship-owner's daughter. Berger had hit the photographer with a flashgun and the photographer had hit back. Tina had screamed and Connery had gone into action, pulling them apart, admittedly with some help from a couple of bodyguards who were with the stars' party. Berger, it was said, hated pressmen. Connery needed picture snatchers like a moose needed a hatstand.

After that he had gone to Almeria for *The Wind and the Lion*, with Candice Bergen, in which he was playing Raisiuli, Sultan of the Berbers and Lord of the Riff, who prayed to Allah five times a day. The critics were caustic about that. One wrote: 'Allah must have been puzzled to hear a sheikh talking with a Scottish accent. He and his Arabs gave me the impression of a stranded touring company of *The Desert Song* waiting to get the show on the road.'

It was in *The Man Who Would Be King*, in which he co-starred with Michael Caine, with John Huston as director, that Connery established himself as a truly fine character actor. As Huston said of Connery and Caine: 'They strike a chord that is unique in my experience.' Huston allowed them to do their own thing but day by day forced them to dig a little deeper into themselves than they had ever done before. And from Connery he extracted an extraordinary performance. Critics conceded that he had buried his Bond image for ever. Yet the lure of Bond persisted.

In September 1975 Connery went to Ireland, to Kevin McClory's home at Straffen House in Co. Kildare, where with a number of other stars he was supporting a charity for handicapped children. It was there that McClory, who had produced *Thunderball*, came up with a proposition for another Bond picture. McClory says: 'I knew Sean didn't want to play Bond again but he knows more about Bond than anyone else and he has a vast number of ideas about what Bond can do.'

McClory was planning an epic called *James Bond and the Secret Service* and persuaded Connery to team up with thriller writer Len Deighton and himself to write the script. The story would once again take them to the Bahamas and Connery was enthused by the prospect of becoming a professional writer. But it was an idea that was to plunge them into almost continuous litigation over a number of years with Cubby Broccoli and his cohorts who were continuing to make Bond films with Roger Moore. Harry Saltzman was no longer involved. He had decided to part company with Cubby and opt out of the Bond bonanza. The news that he had sold out his share of Bond to United Artists for a reported £17.5 million had sped like an arrow to the heart of Sean Connery; it reinforced his views about those who lived off the backs of creative people.

Just before going to Ireland Connery had been involved in a film called *The Death of Robin Hood* (it later became *Robin and Marian*), in which he was playing a poverty-stricken Robin to Audrey Hepburn's Maid Marian. Then, while in Ireland, he began work on *The Next Man*, a political thriller in which he played a Saudi Arabian minister of state who startles the United Nations by proposing peace between Arabs and Israelis and becomes the target of a beautiful professional assassin played by model turned actress Cornelia Sharpe. The film took him to New York where he was joined by Micheline before going on holiday to the Bahamas with their children. While he was in New York a woman columnist ripped into his romantic leading lady in print, claiming she only had the part because she was the girlfriend of the producer. Connery went into action. He phoned the columnist direct and threatened to shove what she had said down her throat. 'She was speechless,' he said later. He was not bothered whether the allegation was true or not. 'That's not the point,' he said. 'She was entitled to say what she felt about the girl's performance but not why she got the part.'

It was the kind of instant reaction that reinforced Connery's reputation as a man's man, particularly among women, although he was never quite sure what they meant by the term. 'I don't think the day will ever come when I do not turn my head to look at an attractive woman,' he says, 'but if being a man's man means someone who enjoys the company of men, then I suppose I am. I enjoy playing golf with my men friends, playing poker and sitting in a bar or my study drinking with men friends. I think men are simpler than women, less devious. Men tend to be more gullible and naive. But then there are a number of women who also prefer the company of men, not just on the sexual level, but because for them to be in the company of women all the time in a strange way breeds more treachery. I think women have a facility for treachery.'

If Connery is a man's man in that sense, then Micheline Connery is a man's woman. 'She sees nothing chauvinistic in the fact that I prefer to play golf with men rather than herself. I think she regards it as a rather Scottish quirk. The French are very pragmatic, you know. She reckons that if I'm out on the course all day with other men there's not very much I can get up to or down to – unless we're all queer, of course. She thinks the business of a bar for men only is very funny. In France men like to be with women much more than we do.'

Micheline Connery was not yet wise in the ways of the film world. She had no experience of the wheeling and dealing that went on behind the scenes and she had no pretensions to becoming an actress, no desire to be in the limelight as the woman who had captured a superstar. She described herself as French *bourgeosie*, and perhaps that gave her the edge when it came to feminine intuition. And of all the women Sean Connery had known, he trusted Micheline. He respected her opinions and judgment, and what is more, he listened to her.

It was a small, an almost silly thing that alerted her suspicions that all was not well with her husband's financial set-up. 'It happened when we moved to our home in Spain,' she says. 'The removal of the furniture from our Embankment flat was entrusted to my husband's representative in London.' This was a man called Kenneth Richards, a film company accountant who had been introduced to Sean Connery in 1972 and had become his business adviser. He lived in Switzerland.

'Everything was fine except for a washing machine that didn't arrive. I asked Mr Richards what had happened and he told me he had given it to his son as a wedding present because it wouldn't work in Spain as the power supply was different. It made me wonder and I went on to investigate. It was the worst moment of my life when I discovered my suspicions were correct.' There was much more at stake than a washing machine. Connery's money had been used to make a series of unsecured property deals in France.

In 1977 Sean Connery asked his wife to go to Switzerland and act on his behalf while he was filming. 'I went to Richards,' says Micheline, 'and asked to be shown the books. He said he did not have any and told me he knew nothing of any property deals.'

A nightmare of litigation lay ahead and the pressures on Sean Connery as he continued to work in film after film were enormous. 'No one except my wife knows the strain of the past few years,' he says now.

He was by this time a resident of Monaco for tax purposes but he continued to live in Marbella, which was pleasant but also presented problems in that he missed conversation and stimulus. He also missed out on what was really going on in the film industry. He had signed early to play Major General Urquhart in *A Bridge Too Far* and it came as a shock when Micheline read in the newspaper just how much some of the Hollywood heavies who had signed were getting. Robert Redford, for example, was reported to have negotiated a fee of $2 million. At first he thought it a mistake but later it was confirmed. He had thought his own salary, to which he had agreed, had been fair for the work he was supposed to do on the picture but when he discovered how much the others were getting for the same amount of work and no more ability he went to the producer Joe Levine and demanded more money. His salary was increased by 50 per cent.

He was not exactly broke, but the millions he thought he possessed were at this time figures on pieces of paper. He had no idea how much he was really worth and meanwhile he wanted all he could get.

In January 1978 Sean Connery and Michael Caine sued a Hollywood studio for £200,000, claiming the money was due to them from *The Man Who Would Be King*. They were due to receive 10 per cent of the gross profits of the picture. The studio replied by launching a $21.5 million suit for 'defamation and malicious interference'. Their claim stemmed from remarks which had been made by Connery in an interview published in *The New York Times* in a general report of what was called 'the new corruption in Hollywood'. Connery had spoken of unjustified costs piled on to a film so as to avoid having to distribute profits. Affidavits piled up like a fall of snow and although in the end they got their money Connery says it cost him £20,000 to do it.

In June 1978 Connery was again being sued, this time over money paid to him for thirteen films, including four starring him as James Bond. The writ was issued by Kenneth Richards and a Liechtenstein company, who claimed a percentage of his earnings.

It was not Connery's style to wilt under pressure, but these events explain why he became a virtual recluse when not filming. Journalists sent to Spain to obtain in-depth interviews from him when he was making *Cuba* on seedy locations in Cadiz and Seville found him declining an informal evening drink with them and clear indications that a pre-arranged round of golf was far more important to him. There was some uneasy communication between takes, and then, work over for the day, he would drive straight home to Marbella in his Mercedes.

It was on that picture that he learned he was embattled on another legal front. Cubby Broccoli and Co. had taken action to kill any rival James Bond picture at birth.

Connery decided he had to return to a basic rule: if he needed a lawyer to understand the words and an accountant to compute the figures, then somebody was trying to hide something. 'There was a time when you could do it on a handshake,' he said. 'Now you agree something with somebody and the first thing he does is turn to his lawyer and say: "For Christ's sake get me out of this." It has become a very fine art being able to put something on paper to read one way while in fact it means something else. It's become a big game, with corporate lawyers lined up against each other. The flak's understandable because there is a great deal of money involved, so now I stand back from the situation. I've told my lawyers that when they've sorted it out to let me know. I still want to do the Bond picture.'

Hollywood has always admired Sean Connery for his style and panache. He was the only British actor to be voted among the Top Ten by the women's organization Weight Watchers Inc., which every year came up with a list of men their members most admired. According to them Connery was 'intriguing, smooth, urbane, with *savoir faire* and class'.

He felt none of these qualities after a hard day's filming but he knew he was bankable and he had been steadily working on one picture after another, although he had had his share of disappointments. His more recent ones, such as *The First Great Train Robbery, Meteor* and *Cuba*, had done less than well but he was constantly in demand.

He had bought a flat in Los Angeles because Hollywood was a good place to be when you were working and he preferred Los Angeles to New York. He had also taken a house off the Bayswater Road in London, where he was due to make *Outland*, a $12-million film with a *High Noon* theme in which he would play a sheriff's role at a space station. He regretted having sold his flat on the Embankment before he had left England. He had asked £95,000 for it but he had been happy to get £60,000. By now it would have been worth £300,000.

He had resigned his directorship of the private bank Dunbar and Co., although he still held 80,000 shares in it, but he was in business as an investor with several U.S. banks in the mid-West and a 600-acre pig and cattle farm in Iowa. He thought it might be a good idea for the two boys Jason and Stefan to spend a few days there.

His long-discussed role of James Bond in the Kevin McClory version, which now had the title *Warhead*, had been shelved. The stumbling block was the threat of drawn-out litigation from Broccoli and United Artists. McClory, who in a court battle had won the right to use the Bond name because of *Thunderball*, had frequently announced Connery would play the part although he had no thought of appearing when he first worked on the script with Len Deighton. It was Micheline who had suggested it might be fun for him to try again but it was difficult to see how the legal deadlock could be overcome and it was becoming too expensive to try.

21

Never Say Never Again

The phrase that came into Sean Connery's mind as he drove the long and glistening black Daimler limousine through the streets of Edinburgh with his family in the back came from Thomas Wolfe. It was the one familiar to all expatriates: 'You can't go home again.' And it was true. The roots were still there: the old school, a monstrously ugly Victorian building; the patch of stubbly grass where he had once played football; the grimy thoroughfares where he had delivered milk and newspapers and later gunned his first motorbike. They had not changed; but he, undoubtedly, had.

A few years before, in 1976, he had taken his wife Micheline, his son Jason, who was then thirteen, and his stepson Stefan, who was twelve, to visit his birthplace. It had been the first visit he had been allowed to his country to spend a few of the ninety days he was entitled to as a tax exile and he had wanted them to see and perhaps understand what had gone into moulding his own attitudes and behaviour over the years. 'I thought seeing the place where I was born might explain a few things to them,' he said, 'and I had brought my mother along, too.

'The place was still a dump with no hot water, four flats sharing two toilets, gas mantles on the landings. And what fascinated me was their individual reaction. Micheline was shocked by the conditions. 'What a dreadful, dreadful place,' she said. My stepson thought it was awful, too. My own son, on the other hand, thought it was interesting and my mother thought it quite nice.'

Denis Selinger says: 'Sean would like to forget his past, but he cannot, perhaps because it is very important to him. It is something he likes to keep at a distance from other people unless he's talking over poverty-stricken old times with mates like Michael Caine who came from a similar background in London and can joke about it.'

Sean Connery says: 'My problem was poverty. The boys' problem is being the sons of a film star. It is something they will have to negotiate and learn how to handle by themselves.' He considered it a matter of individual responsibility. They might see problems from different viewpoints but it came down to the same thing in the end. On a simplistic level he took responsibility for cleaning his own golf clubs. He did not expect anyone else to do it for him just because he was a film star. It was one of the reasons why he sent young Jason to Gordounstoun.

Now, five years later, in August 1981, the boys knew what it was like being the sons of a superstar as they drove through Edinburgh to the European premiere of his film *Outland*. Pipers were waiting for him outside the cinema, young girls massed in a crush broke away when they saw him and came running towards him with outstretched autograph books, and the applause from the audience welled up again and again for this man, immaculate in dinner jacket and black tie for the occasion, who handled the proceedings with wit and warmth.

Perhaps it had something to do with his undoubted sex appeal for the young girls who looked adoringly at the deep-etched lines of worldly experience on his face as he talked to them softly in that Scottish voice. And perhaps it had something to do with his passion for Scotland which, even after seven years as an exile, was still as strong as ever.

Whatever it was, the Scottish International Education Trust would benefit. All the proceeds from the premiere would go into the fund. In ten years the money from the Trust had helped to create a chair of drama at Strathclyde University, helped to educate and promote young Scots with varied talents, and sought to improve industrial relations between men and management. Connery was still investing in Scotland and its people. And working just as hard as ever he did. He had just played, for all his aversion to the breed, a trouble-shooting journalist in a Richard Brooks film called *Wrong Is Right*, and he had flown into Edinburgh for this premiere straight from filming *Maiden Maiden* later renamed *Five Days One Summer*, a Fred Zinneman movie which was being made in the Swiss Alps.

His first move when he stepped from the eight-seater Cessna Citation II private jet which had flown him 1,000 miles from the Val Forno glacier to Edinburgh airport was to go with his brother Neil to the hospital where his mother was ill, having suffered a stroke.

This visit to Edinburgh had been planned in advance, taking into account his ninety-day allowance, and he had a full diary. The disturbing thought was that had he run out of his allowance he could only have gone to his mother's sickbed by laying himself open to tax on his entire earnings for a year. After the hospital he went on to Gleneagles where he was due to play in a pro-celebrity game with Lee Trevino. With so little time available he planned every minute.

Later in the year, in November 1981, he had to come out of tax exile again to fight the High Court claim brought against him by Kenneth Richards, who was seeking a formidable share of his fortune. The Swiss-based accountant and his Liechtenstein company, Films and Properties Establishment, alleged that Connery owed him 2 per cent of his earnings from thirteen films, including *Goldfinger, Thunderball, You Only Live Twice* and *Diamonds Are Forever*. Richards also claimed damages after being dismissed by Connery in December 1977. Sean Connery counter-claimed with allegations of negligence in the handling of his business affairs and breach of duty.

The case was expected to last ten days, but on the fourth day of cross-examination by Connery's counsel Richards decided not to continue and he conceded the counter-claim that he had been negligent. The court heard how a letter sent by Richards to Sean Connery suggested that he might go to jail if certain matters came to the attention of the Inland Revenue and the judge said that Richards' case was totally destroyed.

The strain of the case took its toll of Sean Connery. He said later: 'I was betrayed by a man I trusted. No one knows the pressures I have been under. What made matters worse was that when the case eventually came to court the man I had thought of as a friend tried to blame my wife and make her the villain of the piece.'

Micheline said: 'When I started to investigate what was going on I discovered that Richards had been to my desk and taken out private letters and papers, some of them from Sean. He had photocopied them and then replaced the originals. I believe he was hoping to find something . . . that I had a secret lover. I was shocked.'

Sean Connery said the significance of his counter-claim lay in the sums of money involved. 'His claim against me was a trivial sum compared with what he owes me. Now it's up to me to take legal steps to get it back.'

On 25 May 1982 the High Court awarded Connery £1 million interim payment against his former financial manager who was given twenty-one days to pay it. 'I'll only be happy when I see the money,' Connery said. 'Who knows? He may surprise everybody.' When the full damages are eventually assessed it was believed that Richards might well have to pay Connery up to £2 million.

In August 1982 he was back in Scotland to play in a pro-am tournament at Turnberry. The hospitality flowed freely as usual, with a sponsor picking up all the tabs and a B.B.C. team filming it for television screening in the winter. Connery was faintly amused by the thought that probably more people had watched him play in pro-celebrity golf matches than had ever seen his films. With him was his wife Micheline, a tiny figure by his side, and he felt himself a lucky man. He loved the Scottish landscape and on this course there was a panoramic view of Ailsa Craig and the Mull of Kintyre. In closer perspective were old golfing chums like Bruce Forsyth who was recapturing his youth with the aid of a toupee and a young girl in her twenties in tow.

The organizers thought Connery might be teamed up with the American actor David Soul, but having taken one look at the fellow's golf he said: 'I'm not playing with that bugger.' The vivacious Micheline, who can tell wickedly rude jokes very well indeed, explained: 'Sean's a terrible loser, but you know what they say. Show me a good loser and I'll show you a loser.'

Sean Connery always set out to be a winner. He played with Michael Medwin and Albert Finney, who also had had a late introduction to golf but was coming along famously playing off 18. Such considerations were of some significance when you were having side-bets of as much as £1,000 on a game, or £500 a corner in a four-ball match. He and Finney beat the pros 3 and 2. Yes, Scotland *was* a marvellous country. The only trouble was he had to pick his ninety days carefully to fit these occasions in with his work.

He was back in Spain with his son Jason on holiday when the news was officially announced that, after seven years with lawyers crawling out of the woodwork, he would be playing James Bond one more time. At the age of fifty-two. He rather liked the title, too. It had the right touch of irony. It was *Never Say Never Again*.

Films

Date and place (GB – Great Britain; US – United States) given after each title refer to the making, not the release, of the film.

NO ROAD BACK
(GB 1956)

Director: Montgomery Tully.
Production: Gibraltar.
Producer: Steve Pallos.
Distributor: RKO Radio.
Cast: Skip Homeier, Paul Carpenter, Patricia Dainton, Norman Wooland, Margaret Rawlings, Eleanor Summerfield, Alfie Bass, Sean Connery.

HELL DRIVERS
(GB 1957)

Director: C. Baker Endfield (Cy Endfield).
Production: Aqua Film.
Producer: S. Benjamin Fisz.
Distributor: Jarfid.
Cast: Stanley Baker, Herbert Lom, Peggy Cummins, Patrick McGoohan, William Hartnell, Wilfred Lawson, Sidney James, Jill Ireland, Alfie Bass, Gordon Jackson, Vera Day, Beatrice Varley. Sean Connery was unbilled.

TIME LOCK
(GB 1957)

Director: Gerald Thomas.
Production: Romulus.
Producer: Peter Rogers.
Distributor: Independent/British Lion.
Cast: Robert Beatty, Betty McDowall, Vincent Winter, Lee Patterson, Sandra Francis, Alan Gifford, Robert Ayres, Jack Cunningham. Sean Connery was unbilled.

ACTION OF THE TIGER
(GB 1957)

Director: Terence Young.
Production: Claridge.
Producer: Kenneth Harper.
Distributor: MGM.
Cast: Van Johnson, Martine Carol, Herbert Lom, Gustavo Rocco, Tony Dawson, Anna Gerber, Yvonne Warren, Helen Haye, Sean Connery.

ANOTHER TIME, ANOTHER PLACE
(GB 1958)

Director: Lewis Allen.
Production: Joe Kaufman.
Producers: Lewis Allen, Smedley Aston.
Distributor: Paramount.
Cast: Lana Turner, Barry Sullivan, Glynis Johns, Sean Connery, Sidney James, Terence Longdon, Doris Hare.

DARBY O'GILL AND THE LITTLE PEOPLE
(US 1959)

Director: Robert Stevenson.
Production: Walt Disney.
Producer: Walt Disney.
Distributor: Dyro/Walt Disney.
Cast: Albert Sharpe, Jimmy O'Dea, Janet Munro, Sean Connery, Kieron Moore, Estelle Winwood, Walter Fitzgerald, Dennis O'Dea, J.G. Devlin, Jack MacGowran.

TARZAN'S GREATEST ADVENTURE
(GB 1959)

Director: John Guillermin.
Production: Solar Films.
Producer: Sy Weintraub.
Distributor: Paramount.
Cast: Gordon Scott (as Tarzan), Anthony Quayle, Sara Shane, Sean Connery, Niall MacGinnis, Scilla Gabel, Al Mulock.

THE FRIGHTENED CITY
(GB 1961)

Director: John Lemont.
Production: Zodiac.
Producers: John Lemont and Leigh Vance.
Distributor: Anglo-Amalgamated.
Cast: Herbert Lom, John Gregson, Sean Connery, Alfred Marks, Yvonne Romain, Olive McFarland, Kenneth Griffiths.

ON THE FIDDLE (US: OPERATION SNAFU)
(GB 1961)

Director: Cyril Frankel.
Production: S. Benjamin Fisz.
Producer: S. Benjamin Fisz.
Distributor: Anglo-Amalgamated.
Cast: Alfred Lynch, Sean Connery, Cecil Parker, Norman Rossington, Stanley Holloway, Wilfred Hyde White.

THE LONGEST DAY
(US 1962)

Directors: Ken Annakin (in Britain); Andrew Marton (American exterior episodes); Bernhard Wicki (German episodes); Darryl Zanuck (American interior episodes).
Production: 20th Century Fox.
Producer: Darryl F. Zanuck.
Distributor: 20th Century Fox.
Cast: Richard Burton, Kenneth More, Peter Lawford, Richard Todd, Leo Genn, Michael Medwin, Norman Rossington, John Robinson, Patrick Barr, Donald Houston, Trevor Reid, John

Wayne, Robert Mitchum, Henry Fonda, Robert Ryan, Richard Beymer, Mel Ferrer, Jeffrey Hunter, Sal Mineo, Roddy McDowall, Eddie Albert, Edmond O'Brien, Red Buttons, Henry Grace, Irene Demich, Bourvil, Jean-Louis Barrault, Christian Marquand, Arletty, Madeleine Renaud, Georges Wilson, Fernand Ledoux, Curt Jurgens. Sean Connery was unbilled.

DR NO
(GB 1962)

Director: Terence Young.
Production: Eon.
Producers: Harry Saltzman and Albert R. Broccoli.
Distributor: United Artists.
Cast: Sean Connery, Ursula Andress, Joseph Wiseman, Jack Lord, Anthony Dawson, John Kitzmiller, Zena Marshall, Bernard Lee, Lois Maxwell, Eunice Gayson, Lester Prendergast.

FROM RUSSIA WITH LOVE
(GB 1963)

Director: Terence Young.
Production: Eon.
Producers: Harry Saltzman and Albert R. Broccoli.
Distributor: United Artists.
Cast: Sean Connery, Daniela Bianchi, Pedro Armendariz, Lotte Lenya, Robert Shaw, Bernard Lee, Eunice Gayson, Walter Gotell, Francis de Wolff, George Pastell, Nadja Regin, Lois Maxwell, Aliza Gur, Martine Beeswick, Vladek Sheybal.

WOMAN OF STRAW
(GB 1964)

Director: Basil Dearden.
Production: Novus.
Producer: Michael Relph.
Distributor: United Artists.
Cast: Gina Lollobrigida, Sean Connery, Ralph Richardson, Johnny Sekka, Laurence Hardy, Danny Daniels, A.J. Brown, Peter Madden, Alexander Knox.

MARNIE
(US 1964)

Director: Alfred Hitchcock.
Production: Geoffrey Stanley/Universal International.
Producer: Alfred Hitchcock.
Distributor: Rank.
Cast: Sean Connery, Tippi Hedren, Diane Baker, Martin Gabel, Louise Latham, Bob Sweeney, Alan Napier, S. John Laurer, Mariette Harley, Bruce Dern.

GOLDFINGER
(GB 1964)

Director: Guy Hamilton.
Production: Eon.
Producers: Harry Saltzman and Albert R. Broccoli.
Distributor: United Artists.
Cast: Sean Connery, Honor Blackman, Gert Frobe, Shirley Eaton, Tania Mallet, Harold Sakata, Bernard Lee, Martin Benson, Cec Linder, Austin Willis, Lois Maxwell, Bill Nagy, Alf Joint, Varley Thomas, Nadja Regin.

THE HILL
(GB 1965)

Director: Sidney Lumet.
Production: Seven Arts.
Producer: Kenneth Hyman.
Distributor: MGM.
Cast: Sean Connery, Michael Redgrave, Ian Bannen, Ian Hendry, Harry Andrews, Ossie Davis, Alfred Lynch, Roy Kinnear, Jack Watson, Norman Bird, Neil McCarthy, Howard Goorney, Tony Caunter.

THUNDERBALL
(GB 1965)

Director: Terence Young.
Production: Eon.
Producers: Kevin McClory, Harry Saltzman and Albert R. Broccoli.
Distributor: United Artists.

Cast: Sean Connery, Claudine Auger, Adolfo Celi, Luciana Paoluzzi, Molly Peters, Bernard Lee, Lois Maxwell.

THE INCREDIBLE WORLD OF JAMES BOND
(US 1965)

A David L. Wolper production for United Artists. An hour-long television programme analysing the Bond phenomenon, narrated by Alexander Scourby and consisting of scenes from Bond films.

A FINE MADNESS
(US 1966)

Director: Irvin Kershner.
Production: Pan Arts Co. Inc.
Producer: Jerome Hellman.
Distributor: Warner/Pathé.
Cast: Sean Connery, Joanne Woodward, Jean Seberg.

YOU ONLY LIVE TWICE
(GB 1967)

Director: Lewis Gilbert.
Production: Eon/Danjaq.
Producers: Harry Saltzman and Albert R. Broccoli.
Distributor: United Artists.
Cast: Sean Connery, Akiko Wakabayashi, Tetsuro Tamba, Donald Pleasence, Mie Hama, Karin Dor.

THE BOWLER AND THE BUNNET
(GB 1967)

A film documentary made by Sean Connery for television as a protest against unemployment in Scotland.

SHALAKO
(GB 1968)

Director: Edward Dmytryk.
Production: Kingston Films and Dimitri de Grunwald.
Producer: Euan Lloyd.
Distributor: Warner/Pathé.
Cast: Sean Connery, Brigitte Bardot, Stephen Boyd, Jack Hawkins,

Honor Blackman, Peter Van Eyck, Eric Sykes, Woody Strode, Alexander Knox.

THE MOLLY MAGUIRES
(US 1969)

Director: Martin Ritt.
Production: Tamm.
Producers: Martin Ritt and Walter Bernstein.
Distributor: CIC.
Cast: Sean Connery, Richard Harris, Samantha Eggar, Frank Finlay, Art Lund.

THE RED TENT
(Italy/USSR 1969)

Director: Mikhail K. Kalatozov.
Production: Vides Cinematografica Rome/Mosfilm Moscow.
Producer: Franco Cristaldi.
Distributor: Paramount.
Cast: Sean Connery, Peter Finch, Claudia Cardinale, Hardy Kruger, Mario Adorf, Massimo Girotti, Luigi Vannucchi.

THE ANDERSON TAPES
(US 1971)

Director: Sidney Lumet.
Production: Robert. M. Weitman.
Producer: Robert M. Weitman.
Distributor: Columbia/Warner.
Cast: Sean Connery, Dyan Cannon, Martin Balsam, Ralph Meeker, Christopher Walken.

DIAMONDS ARE FOREVER
(GB 1971)

Director: Guy Hamilton.
Production: Eon/Danjacq.
Producers: Harry Saltzman and Albert R. Broccoli.
Distributor: United Artists.
Cast: Sean Connery, Jill St. John, Lana Wood, Bruce Glover, Patrick Smith, Jimmie Dean.

THE OFFENCE
(GB 1972)

Director: Sidney Lumet.
Production: United Artists/Tantallon.
Producer: Sean Connery.
Distributor: United Artists.
Cast: Sean Connery, Ian Bannen, Trevor Howard, Vivien Merchant.

ZARDOZ
(GB 1973)

Director: John Boorman.
Production: John Boorman/20th Century Fox.
Producer: John Boorman.
Distributor: Fox/Rank.
Cast: Sean Connery, Charlotte Rampling, Sara Kestleman, John Alderton.

RANSOM
(GB 1974)

Director: Casper Wrede.
Production: Lion International.
Producer: Peter Rawley.
Distributor: British Lion.
Cast: Sean Connery, Ian McShane, Norman Bristow, John Cording, Isabel Deab, William Fox.

MURDER ON THE ORIENT EXPRESS
(GB 1974)

Director: Sidney Lumet.
Production: John Brabourne/Richard Goodwin.
Producers: John Brabourne and Richard Goodwin.
Distributor: GW Films for EMI.
Cast: Sean Connery, Ingrid Bergman, Albert Finney, Lauren Bacall, Richard Widmark, Jacqueline Bisset, Sir John Gielgud.

THE WIND AND THE LION
(US 1975)

Director: John Milius.
Production: MGM/Columbia.
Producer: Herb Jaffe.
Distributor: Columbia/Warner.
Cast: Sean Connery, Candice Bergen, Brian Keith, John Huston.

THE MAN WHO WOULD BE KING
(GB 1975)

Director: John Huston.
Production: Allied Artists/Columbia.
Producers: John Foreman and John Huston.
Distributor: Columbia/Warner.
Cast: Sean Connery, Michael Caine, Christopher Plummer, Shakira Caine.

ROBIN AND MARIAN
(US 1976)

Director: Richard Lester.
Production: Rastar Columbia.
Executive producer: Richard Shepherd.
Producer: Denis O'Dell.
Distributor: Columbia/Warner.
Cast: Sean Connery, Audrey Hepburn, Robert Shaw, Nicol Williamson, Richard Harris, Ronnie Barker.

THE NEXT MAN
(US 1976)

Director: Richard Sarafian.
Production: Artists Entertainment Complex.
Executive producer: Emmanuel L. Wolf.
Producer: Martin Bregman.
Distributor: Harris Films.
Cast: Sean Connery, Cornelia Sharpe, Albert Paulsen, Adolfo Celi.

A BRIDGE TOO FAR
(US 1977)

Director: Richard Attenborough.
Production: Joseph Levine Presents Inc.
Producer: Joseph Levine.
Distributor: United Artists.
Cast: Sean Connery, Dirk Bogarde, James Caan, Michael Caine, Elliot Gould, Robert Redford, Gene Hackman, Anthony Hopkins, Hardy Kruger.

THE FIRST GREAT TRAIN ROBBERY (US: THE GREAT TRAIN ROBBERY)
(GB 1978)

Director: Michael Crichton.
Production: Starling Productions.
Producer: John Foreman.
Distributor: United Artists.
Cast: Sean Connery, Lesley Anne Down, Donald Sutherland.

METEOR
(US 1979)

Director: Ronald Neame.
Production: Paladium Pictures.
Executive producers: Sandy Howard and Gabriel Katzka.
Producers: Arnold Orgolini and Theodore Parvin.
Distributor: Columbia/EMI/Warner.
Cast: Sean Connery, Natalie Wood, Karl Malden, Trevor Howard.

CUBA
(US 1979)

Director: Richard Lester.
Production: Holmby Film Corporation.
Producer: Denis O'Dell.
Distributor: United Artists.
Cast: Sean Connery, Brooke Adams, Louisa Moritz, Jack Weston, Martin Balsam, Chris Sarandon.

SEAN CONNERY PROFILE
(GB 1980)

A profile of the actor made by BBC-TV Scotland and transmitted on BBC 1 on 22 December 1981.

OUTLAND
(GB 1981)

Director: Peter Hyams.
Production: Ladd Company.
Executive producer: Stanley O'Toole.
Producer: Richard A. Roth.
Distributor: Columbia/EMI/Warner.
Cast: Sean Connery, Peter Boyle, James Sikking, Kika Markham, Frances Sternhagen.

TIME BANDITS
(GB 1981)

Director: Terry Gilliam.
Production: Handmade Films.
Executive producers: George Harrison and Dennis O'Brien.
Producer: Terry Gilliam.
Distributor: Handmade Films.
Cast: Sean Connery, Shelley Duval, Ian Holm, John Cleese, David Warner, Craig Warwick.

WRONG IS RIGHT
(US 1982)

Director: Richard Brooks.
Production: Rastar.
Producer: Richard Brooks.
Distributor: Columbia.
Cast: Sean Connery, Hardy Kruger, John Saxon, Robert Webber, Katherine Ross.

FIVE DAYS ONE SUMMER
(GB 1982)

Director: Fred Zinneman.
Production: Ladd Company.
Cast: Sean Connery, Betsy Brantley, Lambert Wilson, Anna Massey, Isabel Dean.

NEVER SAY NEVER AGAIN
(Not yet completed)

Director: Irvin Kershner.
Production: Woodcote.
Executive producer: Kevin McClory.
Producer: Jack Schwartzman.
Distributor: Warner.

Index

Action of the Tiger, 29, 42
Acton: home in former convent, 47, 86, 91–2, 98
Adam, Ken, 112
Ali, Muhammed, 85
Allen (Applebaum), Irving, 39, 57
Anderson Tapes, The, 122, 123
Andress, Ursula, 44, 58
Anna Christie, 31, 54
Anna Karenina, 39
Archard, Merry, 26
astrology, 29
Auger, Claudine, 75–6, 77

Baby Doll, 52
Baker, Carroll, 52
Baker, Stanley, 84, 102, 111, 116, 122, 132, 133
Bannen, Ian, 127
Bardot, Brigitte, 101, 102, 104, 107
Barrett, Ray, 122
Bedford, Duchess of, 96
Benny, Jack, 29
Bentall, Michael, 28
Bergen, Candice, 133
Berger, Helmut, 133
Bianchi, Daniela, 56, 60, 61, 93, 94
Big Country, Big Man, 76
Big Knife, 52
Big Tammy (Sean Connery), 11–12
Black Angels, 11
Blackman, Honor, 72
body-building, 21–2; Mr Universe contest, 24

Bond, James (fictional character): creation, 13; Connery takes role, 38–41; Fleming's own self in, 41; gambling system, 50; image-making, 50–1; character, 60; other actors in part, 62, 112, 113, 125, 134; merchandising for, 80; wardrobe, 93
Bond, Sergeant James (policeman), 102–3
Bonyrigg Rose Athletic football team, 19
Bowler and the Bunnet, The, 97
Bradshaw, Harry, 102
Brennan, Archie, 23–4
Bridge, Peter, 95
Bridge Too Far, A, 136
British Legion, 21
Broccoli, Albert R. (Cubby): background, 38–9; making Bond films 38, 48, 61, 65–6, 92, 112, 113, 118; luck, 57–8; partnership with Saltzman, 58; relationship with Connery, 61; breaking bank at Macao, 81; in Japan, 87–9; strong points, 120; litigation with, 134, 137
Brooks, Richard, 140
Bryce, John, 66
burglaries, 47–8, 91–2
Burton, Richard, 73, 83
Buxton Club, 47
Byrne, Ed 'Kooky', 84

Caine, Michael, 134, 137, 139
Caldwell, Ian, 59, 80

Carlisle, Tom, 66, 78
Carol, Martine, 29
Carroll, Ronnie, 79, 84, 116, 122
Carroll, Sue, 57
Casino Royale, 38
Celi, Adolfo, 93
Cilento, Diane: childhood, 36–7; early career, 51–4; voice, 52; first marriage, 37, 52–3; slashing wrists, 53; birth of daughter, 54; divorce from Volpe, 47, 48, 54; meeting with Sean Connery, 31, 54; influence on Connery, 35–6, 96; marriage to Connery, 47, 48; birth of son, 50; view of herself, 58–9; relationship with studio crews, 65; Academy Award nomination, 67; confusion of identities, 69; separation from Connery, 75, 76; rejoins Connery, 76–7; novel writing, 77, 98–9, 116; filming, 83–4; with Connery in Japan, 87; on stage, 110; break-up of marriage to Connery, 115–16; fitting career to Connery's, 116; divorce from Connery, 129
Cilento, Margaret, 47
Clay, Cassius, *see* Ali, Muhammed
Collins, Joan, 95
Connery, Euphemia (Effie; Sean's mother), 13, 17, 73, 139; fortune told, 28–9
Connery, Jason (Sean's son), 75, 99, 124, 138, 139; birth, 50; learning to swim, 65; schooling, 140
Connery, Joseph (Sean's father), 13, 73, 126
Connery, Neil (Sean's brother), 140-1; childhood, 14; views on brother, 17, 28, 73; swimming prank, 23; views on Diane Cilento, 36; in film, 93–4
Connery, Sean (Thomas): astrological chart, 29; character, 17; drinking, 126; earnings, 18, 24, 30, 109, 120, 125, 136–7; earnings from Bond films, 40–1, 61, 67, 92, 113–14, 119, 120; fortune-teller's predictions for, 28-9; handwriting, 100–1; image as man's man, 46; measurements, 43; memory for faces, 70–1; metabolism, 126; professionalism, 64–5; reputation for meanness, 70; smoking, 126; views on men and women, 127, 135

birth, 13; childhood, 13–17; accident as child, 16–17; work as child, 17; schooling, 17; known as Big Tammy, 11–12; work on leaving school, 17–18; joins Royal Navy, 19–21; undertaker, 21; body-building, 21–2, 24; jobs after Royal Navy, 22–4; lifeguard, 23; walk-on stage part, 23; first talking parts in theatre, 24–5; self-education, 27–8; affair with Julie Hamilton, 27, 28, 30–1, 35; television work, 29, 39; film contract with Twentieth-Century Fox, 30; in Hollywood, 32–5; as James Bond, 38–44, 50–1, 56–61, 67, 89–92, 118, 120, 125, 142

demand for privacy about girlfriends, 45–6; meets Diane Cilento, 31, 54; Diane's influence on, 36; marriage to Diane, 47, 48; learns golf, 56, 59, 79; plays in golf tournaments, 80, 102, 108, 111, 116, 133, 142; on golf holidays, 83–4; love of golf, 109, 131; nominations as University Rector, 63, 102, 103

films before Bond, 64; relations with studio crews, 68; attitudes to press, 51, 68–9, 87–90; insistence on privacy, 68–9; fights Bond image, 68–74; separation from Diane, 75, 76; rejoined by Diane, 76–7; voted most popular star, 82, 95, 103, 128

attitude to being thirty-five, 83; views on money, 83, 106; political interests, 94–8, 108–9; in theatre management, 95–6; sues French newspaper, 104–5; sponsors golf tournaments, 108, 109, 114; stage director, 110; return to Bond films, 113–14; as film-maker, 125, 127

break-up of marriage to Diane, 115–16; divorce from Diane, 129; relationship with Micheline Roquebrune, 111, 115, 127, 128, 129, 131;

marriage to Micheline, 131–2; becomes tax exile, 132, 136; business empire, 132–3; financial problems, 135–7
Constantine, Sir Learie, 103
Cooper, Henry, 85, 122
Corbett, Ronnie, 122
Cosman, Stefan, 138, 139
Craigie, Jill, 26, 28
Crane, Cheryl, 32
Creative Management Associates, 129
Crosby, Bing, 108
Cuba, 137, 138

Dahl, Roald, 91
Darby O'Gill and the Little People, 34
Darroch Secondary School, 17
Davis Jnr, Sammy, 46
Dawson, Les, 102
Death of Robin Hood, The, see Robin and Marian
dehydration, 126
Deighton, Len, 134, 138
Diamonds are Forever, 112, 114–15, 118–20, 125, 128
Dixon of Dock Green, 29
Dr No, 38, 39, 43–4, 48, 50, 57, 69, 78
Dors, Diana, 84, 85
Drake, Charlie, 102
drinking, 126
Dunbar and Co., 114, 138
Dunedin Amateur Weight-Lifting Club, 21

East Fife Football Club, 19
Eaton, Shirley, 72
Edinburgh Evening News, 23
Edinburgh School of Art, 22
Edinburgh University: election of rector, 63
Elizabeth, HRH Queen, 101
Elizabeth, HRH Queen (the Queen Mother), 75
Embankment, London: flat, 121, 127, 129, 138
Eon Productions, 38, 66
Evanne, Gillian, 50

Fairfields experiment 96–7
Fenn, Robert, 38
Fetlor Amateurs football club, 18
film-making, 125, 127
Films and Properties Establishment, 141
Finch, Peter, 110
Fine Madness, A, 80, 85, 86, 120
Finney, Albert, 142
First Great Train Robbery, The, 138
First of January, The, 116
Fisz, Ben, 39
Five Days One Summer (Maiden Maiden), 140
Fleming, Ian, 50, 80; creates James Bond, 13; assessment of Connery, 41; court action against, 66; death, 71
Foot, Michael, 26, 28
football, 59; Connery learns to play, 15; teams, 18–19; reproduction of 1876 game, 107
Forsyth, Brue, 79, 84, 122, 124–5, 133, 142
Forsyth, Penny, 124–5
fortune-telling, 28–9
Fountainbridge palais-de-danse, 11, 12
France-Soir, 105
Fraser, Ronnie, 35
From Russia With Love, 50, 56, 59, 60–1, 69, 78

Gail, Zoe, 33
gambling, 50
gang warfare, 11–12
Gardner, Llew, 26, 27, 30, 35, 36
Gavin, John, 112, 113
Gilbert, Lewis, 90
Godfather, The, 119–20
Goldfinger, 59, 65–6, 71–2, 75, 76, 78, 112; golf match, 59, 79
Goldstein, Bob, 29, 30
golf: Connery learns to play, 56, 59, 79; in film, 59, 79; fascination of game, 109, 131; holidays to play, 83–4; tournaments, 80, 102, 108, 111, 116, 142; Connery's personal tournament, 133; in Connery's relation-

ship with Micheline Roquebrune, 131; tournaments sponsored by Connery, 108, 109, 114
Gonzalez, Manolo, 49
Goodman, Lord, 105
Gordonstoun, 140
Grace, Princess of Monaco, 64
Green, Lorne, 29

Hackett, Buddy, 118–19
Hamill, Pete, 68
Hamilton, Guy, 71, 112, 119, 120
Hamilton, Julie, 26–7, 28, 30–1, 35
handwriting, 100–1
Hardy, Robert, 110
Harewood, Lord, 96
Harris, Richard, 104, 107, 129
Hatton, Richard, 40, 76, 113
Hawks, Howard, 39
Hedren, Tippi, 64
Hell Drivers, 29
Henderson, Robert, 27
Hepburn, Audrey, 134
Herman, Ted Allan, 82, 110
Hill, Graham, 116
Hill, Olivia, 50
Hill, The, 72, 78
Hitchcock, Alfred, 64
Hoad, Lew, 101
holidays: Connery's as child, 13, 15–16
Hombre, 83
honeymoon (of Connery and Diane Cilento), 48–9
Hope, Bob, 108
Hopkins, John, 125
Howard, Trevor, 127
Huston, John, 134
Hybrid, The, 116

International Herald Tribune, 105
I've Seen You Cut Lemons, 110

James Bond and the Secret Service (Warhead), 134, 138
Japan: on location in, 89–90; Japanese press, 87–90
Jefford, Barbara, 56
Johns, Glynis, 34

Johnson, Van, 29
Jonathan Cape Ltd, 66
Jong, Erica, 105
Justice, James Robertson, 63

Kazan, Elia, 52
Kennedy, John F., 56
Kenya Open Golf Tournament, 129
King, Alan, 118, 119
Kinnear, Roy, 72
Korda, Alexander, 52

Ladd, Alan, 57, 58
Lazenby, George, 112
Lee, Bernard, 93
Le Grange, Coble, 80
Lenya, Lotte, 60–1
Leopold, King, 108
Lewis, Patricia, 34–5, 39
litigation: libel action, 104–5; over Bond film, 134, 137; over money, 136–8, 141–2
Lloyd, Evan, 104
Lloyd, Sue, 46–7
Logan, Jimmy, 123
Lollobrigida, Gina, 60, 64
Lollobrigida, Gydo, 93
Longest Day, The, 36
Los Angeles: flat, 138
Lumet, Sidney, 72, 123, 127, 133
Lynch, Kenny, 122

Macbeth, 111
McClory, Kevin, 66, 73, 81, 134, 138
McCourt, Malachy, 107
McKern, Leo, 95
McLean, Helen (Connery's grandmother), 15
McNaughton, Ian, 35
Maiden Maiden, see Five Days One Summer
Manipulator, The, 77; 99
Mann, Roderick, 127
Man Who Would Be King, The, 131–2, 133–4, 137
Marbella, 101, 129
Margaret, HRH Princess, 107
Marnie, 64

Mason, Glen, 59, 122
Mau Mau (beach club), 133
Maxwell, Lois, 93, 94
Mayer, Louis B., 119
Medwin, Michael, 84, 102, 122, 142
Menuhin, Yehudi, 63
Merchant, Vivien, 127
Merk, Rosa, 33
Merman, Doc, 76
Meteor, 138
Molly Maguires, The, 104, 107, 109, 126
Monaco, 136
Moore, Bobby, 128
Moore, Roger, 62, 125, 134
Moroccan Golf Championships, 111
Mosley, Leonard, 86
Motion Picture Herald, 69, 82, 103
Munro, Janet, 34
Murder on the Orient Express, 133
Murray, Chic, 123

Nassau: on location in, 76–7
Never Say Never Again, 142
Newman, Paul, 83
New York: Paramount Theatre, 82
Next Man, The, 134
Noble, Peter, 26, 35
No Road Back, 29
Nyerere, Dr Julius, 63

O'Connor, Christy, 102
Offence, The (Something Like The Truth), 127–8
Onassis, Aristotle, 121
Onassis, Tina, 133
On Her Majesty's Secret Service, 112
Operation Kid Brother, 93–4
Outland, 138

Palance, Jack, 29–30
Paluzzi, Luciana, 76, 77
Paola, Princess of Belgium, 108
Picker, David, 113
politics, 96–8, 108
press: in Japan, 87–9; Connery's attitude towards, 51, 68–9, 130, 133
Putney: house, 98, 116–17

Q Theatre, 29

Rakne, Dr Ola, 103
Rakoff, Alvin, 30
Rampling, Charlotte, 129
Ransom, 133
Ratoff, Gregory, 38
Red Beret, 58
Redford, Robert, 136
Red Tent, The, 109–10
Reed, Oliver, 116
Regin, Nadja, 72
Reich, Dr Wilhelm, 103
Requiem for a Heavyweight, 30
Reventlow, Lance, 112
Reynolds, Burt, 129
Richards, Kenneth, 136, 137, 141–2
Ritchie's Restaurant, Edinburgh, 22
Ritt, Martine, 107
Robin and Marian (The Death of Robin Hood), 134
Roquebrune, Micheline, 115; meeting with Connery, 111; living with Connery, 127; relationship with Connery, 128, 129, 131; marriage to Connery, 131–2; as wife of Connery, 134–6, 141, 142
Rossiter, Leonard, 95
Royal and Ancient Golf Club, St Andrews, 116
Royal Navy, 19–21
Russia, *see* Soviet Union

Sabatello, Dorio, 94
Sachs, Gunther, 102
Sailor of Fortune, 29
St Andrews Royal and Ancient Golf Club, 116
St Andrews University: political survey, 108; Rector, 102, 103
St Cuthbert's Co-operative Society, 17
St John, Jill, 112, 113, 119
St Vincent, Italy, 50
Sakata, Harold, 66
Saltzman, Harry: strong points, 120; partnership with Broccoli, 58; makes Bond films, 38, 48, 61, 65–6, 92, 94, 112, 118; relationship with Connery,

61, 113; sells share in Bond films, 134
Salvation Army: attack on Bond, 78
Scottish International Education Trust, 98, 114, 121, 122, 140
Scottish Nationalists, 132; Connery as prospective MP for, 108–9
Secret of the World, The, 82
Selinger, Denis, 45, 70, 82, 129, 139
sex: Connery's early introduction to, 22
Seyn, Seyna, 50
Shalako, 101, 104, 107
Sharpe, Cornelia, 134–5
Shaw, Robert, 59, 61, 78
Sigrist, Bobo, 66
Simmons, Bob, 43
Sinclair, Anthony, 42–3
Sixty Glorious Years, 23
Something Like the Truth (The Offence), 127–8
Sopel, Stanley, 38, 39, 40–1, 42, 58, 66, 89, 113, 120; opinion of Connery, 70
Soul, David, 142
South Pacific, 24–5, 27
souvenirs of Bond, 80
Soviet Union, 78, 109–10
Spain: as tax haven, 132
speeding offence, 102–3
Stewart, Sir Iain, 96–7, 101, 114, 116, 128
Stompanato, Johnny, 32–3
Strathclyde University, 140
stunts, 43, 57
swimming, 23; Connery teaches son, 65
Sykes, Eric, 84, 102, 116

Tantallon, 125
Tarbuck, Jimmy, 122, 133
Tatham, Jeremy, 129
tax exile, 132, 136
Taylor, Elizabeth, 83
television work, 29, 39
theatre management, 95–6
This Story is Yours, 125
Thunderball, 66, 73, 75, 76, 81, 95
Tich (horse), 18
Tiger at the Gates, 52

Time Lock, 29
Tokyo, 87–9
Tom Jones, 67
Trevino, Lee, 141
Truth About Women, The, 53
'Truth or Consequences' (game), 84–5
Turner, Lana, 32–3, 34, 35
Twentieth-Century Fox, 30
Tyan, Kenneth, 125

United Artists, 125, 134
Ustinov, Peter, 63

Valdor gang, 11–12
Variety (newspaper), 120
Vatican: attack on Bond, 78
Volpe, Andrea, 37, 52–3
Volpe, Giovanna Margaret, 54, 75, 124
Volpone, 95

Warhead (James Bond and the Secret Service), 134, 138
Warner, Jack L., 119, 120
Warwick Films, 39, 58
Weight Watchers Inc: Top Ten Men, 138
Whicker, Alan, 87–9
White, Michael, 60
Whittingham, Jack, 66
Williams, Andy, 108
Wilson, Harold, 105
Wind and the Lion, The, 133
Winters, Shelley, 46, 82
Woman of Straw, 60, 64
Wood, Lana, 112
Woodward, Joanne, 86
Wrede, Caspar, 133
Wrong is Right, 140

Young, Terence, 39, 42, 55, 56, 60, 62, 68, 80
You Only Live Twice, 82, 90–1, 92, 101–2, 126

Zanuck, Darryl F., 119
Zardoz, 129
Zinneman, Fred, 140
Zuleika, 53